The Jerusalem Sinner Saved

Or, Good News for the Vilest of Men

John Bunyan

The Jerusalem Sinner Saved; or, Good News for the Vilest of Men

The present edition is a reproduction of previous publication of this classic work. Minor typographical errors may have been corrected without note; however, for an authentic reading experience the spelling, punctuation, and capitalization have been retained from the original text.

ISBN: 979-8-88830-269-9

THE
JERUSALEM SINNER SAVED
OR
GOOD NEWS FOR THE VILEST OF MEN

BEGINNING AT JERUSALEM.—Luke xxiv 47

The whole verse runs thus: "And that repentance and remission of sins should be preached in his name among all nations, beginning at Jerusalem."

The words were spoken by Christ, after he rose from the dead, and they are here rehearsed after an historical manner, but do contain in them a formal commission, with a special clause therein. The commission is, as you see, for the preaching of the gospel, and is very distinctly inserted in the holy record by Matthew and Mark. "Go teach all nations," &c. "Go ye into all the world, and preach the gospel unto every creature." Matt. xxviii. 19; Mark xvi. 15. Only this cause is in special mentioned by Luke, who saith, That as Christ would have the doctrine of repentance and remission of sins preached in his name among all nations, so he would have the people of Jerusalem to have the first proffer thereof. Preach it, saith Christ, in all nations, but begin at Jerusalem.

The apostles then, though they had a commission so large as to give them warrant to go and preach the gospel in all the world, yet by this clause they were limited as to the beginning of their ministry: they were to begin this work at Jerusalem. "Beginning at Jerusalem."

Before I proceed to an observation upon the words, I must (but briefly) touch upon two things: namely,

I. Show you what Jerusalem now was.

II. Show you what it was to preach the gospel to them.

I. For the first, Jerusalem is to be considered, either,

1. With respect to the descent of her people: or,

2. With respect to her preference and exaltation: or,

3. With respect to her present state, as to her decays.

First, As to her descent: she was from Abraham, the sons of Jacob, a people that God singled out from the rest of the nations to set his love upon them.

Secondly, As to her preference or exaltation, she was the place of God's worship, and that which had in and with her the special tokens and signs of God's favour and presence, above any other people in the world. Hence the tribes went up to Jerusalem to worship; there was God's house, God's high-priest, God's sacrifices accepted, and God's eye, and God's heart perpetually; Psalm lxxvi. 1, 2; Psalm cxxii.; 1 Kings ix. 3. But,

Thirdly, We are to consider Jerusalem also in her decays; for as she is so considered, she is the proper object of our text, as will be further showed by and by.

Jerusalem, as I told you, was the place and seat of God's worship, but now decayed, degenerated, and apostatized. The word, the rule of worship, was rejected of them, and in its place they had put and set up their own traditions; they had rejected also the most weighty ordinances, and put in the room thereof their own little things, Matt. xv.; Mark vii. Jerusalem was therefore now greatly backsliding, and become the place where truth and true religion were much defaced.

It was also now become the very sink of sin and seat of hypocrisy, and gulf where true religion was drowned. Here also now reigned presumption, and groundless confidence in God, which is the bane of souls. Amongst its rulers, doctors, and leaders, envy, malice, and blasphemy vented itself against the power of godliness, in all places where it was espied; as also against the promoters of it; yea, their Lord and Maker could not escape them.

In a word, Jerusalem was now become the shambles, the very slaughter-shop for saints. This was the place wherein the prophets, Christ, and his people, were most horribly persecuted and murdered. Yea, so hardened at this time was this Jerusalem in her sins, that she feared not to commit the biggest, and to bind herself by wish under the guilt and damning evil of it; saying, when she had murdered the Son of God, "His blood be upon us and our children."

And though Jesus Christ did, both by doctrine, miracles, and holiness of life, seek to put a stop to their villanies, yet they shut their eyes, stopped their ears, and rested not, till, as was hinted before, they had driven him out of the world. Yea, that they might, if possible, have extinguished his name, and exploded his doctrine out of the world, they, against all argument, and in despite of Heaven, its mighty hand, and undeniable proof of his resurrection, did hire soldiers to invent a lie, saying, his disciples stole him away from the grave; on purpose that men might not count him the Saviour of the world, nor trust in him for the remission of sins.

They were, saith Paul, contrary to all men: for they did not only shut up the door of life against themselves, but forbade that it should be opened to any else. "Forbidding us," saith he, "to preach to the Gentiles, that they might be saved, to fill up their sins alway;" Matt. xxiii. 35; chap. xv. 7–9; Mark vii. 6–8; Matt. iii. 7–9; John viii. 33, 41; Matt. xxvii. 18; Mark iii. 30; Matt. xxiii. 37; Luke xiii. 33, 34; Matt. xxvii. 25; chap. xx. 11–16; 1 Thess. ii. 14–16.

This is the city, and these are the people; this is their character, and these are their sins: nor can there be produced their parallel in all this world. Nay, what world, what people, what nation, for sin and transgression, could, or can be compared to Jerusalem! especially if you join to the matter of fact the light they sinned against, and the patience which they abused. Infinite was the wickedness upon this account which they committed.

After all their abusings of wise men, and prophets, God sent unto them John Baptist, to reduce them, and then his Son to redeem them; but they would be neither reduced nor redeemed, but persecuted both to the death. Nor did they, as I said, stop here; the holy apostles they afterwards persecuted also to death, even so many as they could; the rest they drove from them unto the utmost corners.

II. I come now to show you what it was to preach the gospel to them. It was, saith Luke, "to preach to them repentance and remission of sins" in Christ's name; or, as Mark has it, to bid them "repent and believe the gospel," Mark i. 15; not that repentance is a cause of remission, but a sign of our hearty reception thereof. Repentance is therefore here put to intimate, that no pretended faith of the gospel is good that is not accompanied with it: and this he doth on purpose, because he would not have them deceive themselves: for with what faith can he expect remission of sins in the name of Christ, that is not heartily sorry for them? Or how shall a man be able to give to others a satisfactory account of his unfeigned subjection to the gospel, that yet abides in his impenitency?

Wherefore repentance is here joined with faith in the way of receiving the gospel. Faith is that without which it cannot be received at all; and repentance that without which it cannot be received unfeignedly. When therefore Christ says, he would have repentance and remission of sins preached in his name among all nations, it is as much as to say, I will that all men every where be sorry for their sins, and accept of mercy at God's hand through me, lest they fall under his wrath in the judgment. For as I had said, without repentance, what pretence soever men have of faith, they cannot escape the wrath to come. Wherefore Paul saith, God commands "all men every where to repent," (in order to their salvation), "because he hath appointed a day in the which he will judge the world in righteousness by that man whom he hath ordained;" Acts xvii. 31.

And now to come to this clause, "Beginning at Jerusalem;" that is, that Christ would have Jerusalem have the first offer of the gospel.

1. This cannot be so commanded, because they had now any more right of themselves thereto than had any of the nations of the world; for their sins had divested them of all self-deservings.

2. Nor yet, because they stood upon the advance-ground with the worst of the sinners of the nations; nay, rather, the sinners of the nations had the advance-ground of them: for Jerusalem was, long before she had added this iniquity to her sin, worse than the very nations that God cast out before the children of Israel; 2 Chron. xxxiii.

3. It must therefore follow, that this clause, Begin at Jerusalem, was put into this commission of mere grace and compassion, even from the overflowings of the bowels of mercy; for indeed they were the worst, and so in the most deplorable condition of any people under the heavens.

Whatever, therefore, their relation was to Abraham, Isaac, or Jacob, however they formerly had been the people among whom God had placed his name and worship, they were now degenerated from God, more than the nations were from their idols, and were become guilty of the highest sins which the people of the world were capable of committing. Nay, none can be capable of committing of such pardonable sins as they committed against their God, when they slew his Son, and persecuted his name and word.

From these words, therefore, thus explained, we gain this observation:

That Jesus Christ would have mercy offered in the first place to the biggest sinners.

That these Jerusalem sinners were the biggest sinners that ever were in the world, I think none will deny, that believes that Christ was the best man that ever was in the world, and also was their Lord God. And that they were to have the first offer of his grace, the text is as clear as the sun; for it saith, "Begin at Jerusalem." "Preach," saith he, "repentance and remission of sins" to the Jerusalem sinners: to the Jerusalem sinners in the first place.

One would a-thought, since the Jerusalem sinners were the worst and greatest sinners, Christ's greatest enemies, and those that not only despised his person, doctrine, and miracles, but that a little before had had their hands up to the elbows in his heart-blood, that he should rather have said, Go into all the world, and preach repentance and remission of sins among all nations; and after that offer the same to Jerusalem; yea, it had been infinite grace, if he had said so. But what grace is this, or what name shall we give it, when he commands that this repentance and remission of sins, which is designed to be preached in all nations, should first be offered to Jerusalem, in the first place to the worst of sinners!

Nor was this the first time that the grace which was in the heart of Christ thus shewed itself to the world. For while he was yet alive, even while he was yet in Jerusalem, and perceived even among these Jerusalem sinners, which was the most vile amongst them, he still in his preaching did signify that he had a desire that the worst of these worst should in the first place come unto him. The which he showeth, where he saith to the better sort of them, "The publicans and harlots enter into the kingdom of God before you;" Matt. xxi. 31. Also when he compared Jerusalem with the sinners of the nations, then he commands that the Jerusalem sinners should have the gospel at present confined to them. "Go not," saith he, "into the way of the Gentiles, and into any of the cities of the Samaritans enter ye not; but go rather to the lost sheep of the house of Israel;" Matt. x. 5, 6; chap. xxiii. 37; but go rather to them, for they were in the most fearful plight.

These therefore must have the cream of the gospel, namely, the first offer thereof in his lifetime: yea, when he departed out of the world, he left this as part of his last will with his preachers, that they also should offer it first to Jerusalem. He had a mind, a careful mind, as it seems, to privilege the worst of sinners with the first offer of mercy, and to take from among them a people to be the first fruits unto God and to the Lamb.

The 15th of Luke also is famous for this, where the Lord Jesus takes more care, as appears there by three parables, for the lost sheep, lost groat, and the prodigal son, than for the other sheep, the other pence, or for the son that said he had never transgressed, yea, he shows that there is joy in heaven, among the angels of God, at the repentance of one sinner, more than over ninety and nine just persons, which need no repentance; Luke xv.

After this manner therefore the mind of Christ was set on the salvation of the biggest sinners in his lifetime. But join to this, this clause, which he carefully put into the apostles' commission to preach, when he departed hence to the Father, and then you shall see that his heart was vehemently set upon it; for these were part of his last words with them, Preach my gospel to all nations, but see that you begin at Jerusalem.

Nor did the apostles overlook this clause when their Lord was gone into heaven: they went first to them of Jerusalem, and preached Christ's gospel to them: they abode also there for a season and time, and preached it to no body else, for they had regard to the commandment of their Lord.

And it is to be observed, namely, that the first sermon which they preached after the ascension of Christ, it was preached to the very worst of these Jerusalem sinners, even to these that were the murderers of Jesus Christ, Acts ii. 23, for these are part of the sermon: "Ye took him, and by wicked hands have crucified and slain him." Yea, the next sermon, and the next, and also the next to that, was preached to the self-same murderers, to the end they might be saved; Acts iii. 14–16; chap. iv. 10, 11; chap. v. 30; chap. vii. 52.

But we will return to the first sermon that was preached to these Jerusalem sinners, by which will be manifest more than great grace, if it be duly considered.

For after that Peter, and the rest of the apostles, had, in their exhortation, persuaded these wretches to believe that they had killed the Prince of life, and after they had duly fallen under the guilt of their murder, saying, "Men and brethren, what shall we do?" he replies, by an universal tender to them all in general, considering them as Christ's killers, that if they were sorry for what they had done, and would be baptized for the remission of their sins in his name, they should receive the gift of the Holy Ghost; Acts ii. 37, 38.

This he said to them all, though he knew that they were such sinners. Yea, he said it without the least stick or stop, or pause of spirit, as to whether he had best to say so or no. Nay, so far off was Peter from making an objection against one of them, that by a particular clause in his exhortation, he endeavours, that not one of them may escape the salvation offered. "Repent," saith he, "and be baptized every one of you." I shut out never a one of you; for I am commanded by my Lord to deal with you, as it were, one by one, by the word of his salvation. But why speaks he so particularly? Oh! there were reasons for it. The people with whom the apostles were now to deal, as they were murderers of our Lord, and to be charged in the general with his blood, so they had their various and particular acts of villany in the guilt thereof, now lying upon their consciences. And the guilt of these their various and particular acts of wickedness, could not perhaps be reached to a removal thereof, but by this particular application. Repent every one of you; be baptized every one of you, in his name, for the remission of sins, and you shall, every one of you, receive the gift of the Holy Ghost.

Object. But I was one of them that plotted to take away his life. May I be saved by him?

Peter. Every one of you.

Object. But I was one of them that bare false witness against him. Is there grace for me?

Peter. For every one of you.

Object. But I was one of them that cried out, Crucify him, crucify him; and desired that Barabbas the murderer might live, rather than him. What will become of me, think you?

Peter. I am to preach repentance and remission of sins to every one of you, says Peter.

Object. But I was one of them that did spit in his face when he stood before his accusers. I also was one that mocked him, when in anguish he hanged bleeding on the tree. Is there room for me?

Peter. For every one of you, says Peter.

Object. But I was one of them that in his extremity said, give him gall and vinegar to drink. Why may not I expect the same when anguish and guilt is upon me?

Peter. Repent of these your wickednesses, and here is remission of sins for every one of you.

Object. But I railed on him, I reviled him, I hated him, I rejoiced to see him mocked at by others. Can there be hopes for me?

Peter. There is for every one of you. "Repent and be baptised every one of you in the name of Jesus Christ, for the remission of sins, and ye shall receive the gift of the Holy Ghost." Oh! what a blessed "Every one of you," is here! How willing was Peter, and the Lord Jesus, by his ministry, to catch these murderers with the word of the gospel, that they might be made monuments of the grace of God! How unwilling, I say, was he, that any of these should escape the hand of mercy! Yea, what an amazing wonder it is to think, that above all the world, and above every body in it, these should have the first offer of mercy! "Beginning at Jerusalem."

But was there not something of moment in this clause of the commission? Did not Peter, think you, see a great deal in it, that he should thus begin with these men, and thus offer, so particularly, this grace to each particular man of them?

But, as I told you, this is not all; these Jerusalem sinners must have this offer again and again; every one of them must be offered it over and over. Christ would not take their first rejection for a denial, nor their second repulse for a denial; but he will have grace offered once, and twice, and thrice, to these Jerusalem sinners. Is not this amazing grace? Christ will not be put off. These are the sinners that are sinners indeed. They are sinners of the biggest sort; consequently such as Christ can, if they convert and be saved, best serve his ends and designs upon. Of which more anon.

But what a pitch of grace is this! Christ is minded to amaze the world, and to shew, that he acteth not like the children of men. This is that which he said of old. "I will not execute the fierceness of my wrath, I will not return to destroy Ephraim; for I am God and not man;" Hos. xi. 9. This is not the manner of men; men are shorter winded; men are soon moved to take vengeance, and to right themselves in a way of wrath and indignation. But God is full of grace, full of patience, ready to forgive, and one that delights in mercy. All this is seen in our text. The biggest sinners must first be offered mercy; they must, I say, have the cream of the gospel offered unto them.

But we will a little proceed. In the third chapter we find, that they who escaped converting by the first sermon, are called upon again, to accept of grace and forgiveness, for their murder committed upon the Son of God. You have killed, yea, "you have denied, the holy one and the just, and desired a murderer to be granted unto you; and killed the Prince of life." Mark, he falls again upon the very men that actually were, as you have it in the chapters following, his very betrayers and murderers, Acts iii. 14, 15; as being loath that they should escape the mercy of forgiveness; and exhorts them again to repent, that their sins might "be blotted out;" verses 19, 20.

Again, in the fourth chapter, he charges them afresh with this murder, ver. 10; but withal tells them, salvation is in no other. Then, like a heavenly decoy, he puts himself also among them, to draw them the better under the net of the gospel; saying, "There is none other name under heaven given among men, whereby we must be saved;" ver. 12.

In the fifth chapter you find them railing at him, because he continued preaching among them salvation in the name of Jesus. But he tells them, that that very Jesus whom they had slain and hanged on a tree, him God had raised up, and exalted to be a Prince and a Saviour, to give repentance to Israel, and forgiveness of sins: ver. 29–31. Still insinuating, that though they had killed him, and to this day rejected him, yet his business was to bestow upon them repentance and forgiveness of sins.

'Tis true, after they began to kill again, and when nothing but killing would serve their turn, then they that were scattered abroad went every where preaching the word. Yet even some of them so hankered after the conversion of the Jews, that they preached the gospel only to them. Also the apostles still made their abode at Jerusalem, in hopes that they might yet let down their net for another draught of these Jerusalem sinners. Neither did Paul and Barnabas, who were the ministers of God to the Gentiles, but offer the gospel, in the first place, to those of them that for their wickedness were scattered like vagabonds among the nations; yea, and when they rendered rebellion and blasphemy for their service and love, they replied, it was necessary that the word of God should first have been spoken to them; Acts i. 8; chap. xiii. 46, 47.

Nor was this their preaching unsuccessful among these people: but the Lord Jesus so wrought with the word thus spoken, that thousands of them came flocking to him for mercy. Three thousand of them closed with him at the first; and afterwards two thousand more; for now they were in number about five thousand; whereas before sermons were preached to these murderers, the number of the disciples was not above "a hundred and twenty;" Acts i. 15; chap. ii. 41; chap. iv. 4.

Also among these people that thus flocked to him for mercy, there was a "great company of the priests;" chap. vi. 7. Now the priests were they that were the greatest of these biggest sinners; they were the ringleaders, they were the inventors and ringleaders in the mischief. It was they that set the people against the Lord Jesus, and that were the cause why the uproar increased, until Pilate had given sentence upon him. "The chief priests and elders," says the text, "persuaded (the people) the multitude," that they should ask Barabbas, and destroy Jesus; Matt. xxvii. 20. And yet behold the priests, yea, a great company of the priests, became obedient to the faith.

Oh the greatness of the grace of Christ, that he should be thus in love with the souls of Jerusalem sinners! that he should be thus delighted with the salvation of the Jerusalem sinners! that he should not only will that his gospel should be offered them, but that it should be offered unto them first, and before other sinners were admitted to a hearing of it. "Begin at Jerusalem."

Were this doctrine well believed, where would there be a place for a doubt, or a fear of the damnation of the soul, if the sinner be penitent, how bad a life soever he has lived, how many soever in number are his sins?

But this grace is hid from the eyes of men; the devil hides it from them; for he knows it is alluring, he knows it has an attracting virtue in it: for this is it that above all arguments can draw the soul to God.

I cannot help it, but must let drop another word. The first church, the Jerusalem church, from whence the gospel was to be sent into all the world, was a church made up of Jerusalem sinners. These great sinners were here the most shining monuments of the exceeding grace of God.

Thus you see I have proved the doctrine; and that not only by showing you that this was the practice of the Lord Jesus Christ in his lifetime, but his last will when he went up to God; saying, Begin to preach at Jerusalem.

Yea, it is yet further manifested, in that when his ministers first began to preach there, he joined his power to the word, to the converting of thousands of his betrayers and murderers, and also many of the ringleading priests to the faith.

I shall now proceed, and shall show you,

1. The reasons of the point:

2. And then make some application of the whole.

The observation, you know, is this: Jesus Christ would have mercy offered, in the first place, to the biggest sinners, to the Jerusalem sinners: "Preach repentance, and remission of sins, in my name, among all nations, beginning at Jerusalem."

The reasons of the point are:

First, Because the biggest sinners have most need thereof. He that has most need, reason says, should be helped first. I mean, when a helping hand is offered, and now it is: for the gospel of the grace of God is sent to help the world; Acts xvi. 9. But the biggest sinner has most need. Therefore, in reason, when mercy is sent down from heaven to men, the worst of men should have the first offer of it. "Begin at Jerusalem." This is the reason which the Lord Christ himself renders, why in his lifetime he left the best, and turned him to the worst; why he sat so loose from the righteous, and stuck so close to the wicked. "The whole," saith he, "have no need of the physician, but the sick. I came not to call the righteous, but sinners to repentance;" Mark ii. 15–47.

Above you read, that the scribes and pharisees said to his disciples, "How is it that he eateth and drinketh with publicans and sinners?" Alas! they did not know the reason: but the Lord renders them one, and such an one as is both natural and cogent, saying, These have need, most need. Their great necessity requires that I should be most friendly, and show my grace first to them.

Not that the other were sinless, and so had no need of a Saviour;

but the publicans and their companions were the biggest sinners; they were, as to view, worse than the scribes; and therefore in reason should be helped first, because they had most need of a Saviour.

Men that are at the point to die have more need of the physician than they that are but now and then troubled with an heart-fainting qualm. The publicans and sinners were, as it were, in the mouth of death; death was swallowing of them down: and therefore the Lord Jesus receives them first, offers them mercy first. "The whole have no need of the physician, but the sick. I came not to call the righteous, but sinners to repentance." The sick, as I said, is the biggest sinner, whether he sees his disease or not. He is stained from head to foot, from heart to life and conversation. This man, in every man's judgment, has the most need of mercy. There is nothing attends him from bed to board, and from board to bed again, but the visible characters, and obvious symptoms, of eternal damnation. This therefore is the man that has need, most need; and therefore in reason should be helped in the first place. Thus it was with the people concerned in the text, they were the worst of sinners, Jerusalem sinners, sinners of the biggest size; and therefore such as had the greatest need; wherefore they must have mercy offered to them, before it be offered any where else in the world. "Begin at Jerusalem," offer mercy first to a Jerusalem sinner. This man has most need, he is farthest from God, nearest to hell, and so one that has most need. This man's sins are in number the most, in cry the loudest, in weight the heaviest, and consequently will sink him soonest: wherefore he has most need of mercy. This man is shut up in Satan's hand, fastest bound in the cords of his sins: one that justice is whetting his sword to cut off; and therefore has most need, not only of mercy, but that it should be extended to him in the first place.

But a little further to show you the true nature of this reason, to wit, That Jesus Christ would have mercy offered, in the first place, to the biggest sinners.

First, Mercy ariseth from the bowels and compassion, from pity, and from a feeling of the condition of those in misery. "In his love, and in his pity, he saveth us." And again, "The Lord is pitiful, very pitiful, and of great mercy;" Isa. lxiii. 9; James v. 11.

Now, where pity and compassion is, there is yearning of bowels; and where there is that, there is a readiness to help. And, I say again, the more deplorable and dreadful the condition is, the more directly doth bowels and compassion turn themselves to such, and offer help and deliverance. All this flows from our first scripture proof; I came to call them that have need; to call them first, while the rest look on and murmur.

"How shall I give thee up, Ephraim?" Ephraim was a revolter from God, a man that had given himself up to devilism: a company of men, the ten tribes, that worshipped devils, while Judah kept with his God. "But how shall I give thee up, Ephraim? How shall I deliver thee, Israel? How shall I make thee as Admah? How shall I set thee as Zeboim? (and yet thou art worse than they: nor has Samaria committed half thy sins); Ezek. xvi. 46–51. My heart is turned within me, and my repentings are kindled together;" Hos. xi. 8.

But where do you find that ever the Lord did thus yearn in his bowels for and after any self-righteous man? No, no; they are the publicans and harlots, idolaters and Jerusalem sinners, for whom his bowels thus yearn and tumble about within him: for, alas! poor worms, they have most need of mercy.

Had not the good Samaritan more compassion for that man that fell among thieves (though that fall was occasioned by his going from the place where they worshipped God, to Jericho, the cursed city) than we read he had for any other besides? His wine was for him, his oil was for him, his beast for him; his penny, his care, and his swaddling bands for him; for alas! wretch, he had most need; Luke x. 30–35.

Zaccheus the publican, the chief of the publicans, one that had made himself the richer by wronging of others; the Lord at that time singled him out from all the rest of his brother publicans, and that in the face of many Pharisees, and proclaimed in the audience of them all, that that day salvation was come to his house; Luke xix. 1–8.

The woman also that had been bound down by Satan for eighteen years together, his compassions putting him upon it, he loosed her, though those that stood by snarled at him for so doing; Luke xiii. 11–13,

And why the woman of Sarepta, and why Naaman the Syrian, rather than widows and lepers in Israel, but because their conditions were more deplorable, (for that) they were most forlorn, and farthest from help; Luke iv. 25, 27.

But I say, why all these, thus named? why have we not a catalogue of some holy men that were so in their own eyes, and in the judgment of the world? Alas if at any time any of them are mentioned, how seemingly coldly doth the record of scripture present them to us? Nicodemus, a night professor, and Simon the pharisee, with his fifty pence; and their great ignorance of the methods of grace, we have now and then touched upon.

Mercy seems to be out of his proper channel, when it deals with self-righteous men; but then it runs with a full stream when it extends itself to the biggest sinners. As God's mercy is not regulated by man's goodness, nor obtained by man's worthiness; so not much set out by saving of any such. But more of this anon.

And here let me ask my reader a question: suppose that as thou art walking by some pond side, thou shouldst espy in it four or five children all in danger of drowning, and one in more danger than all the rest, judge which has most need to be helped out first? I know thou wilt say, he that is nearest drowning. Why, this is the case; the bigger sinner, the nearer drowning; therefore the bigger sinner the more need of mercy; yea, of help by mercy in the first place. And to this our text agrees, when it saith, "Beginning at Jerusalem." Let the Jerusalem sinner, says Christ, have the first offer, the first invitation, the first tender of my grace and mercy, for he is the biggest sinner, and so has most need thereof.

Secondly, Christ Jesus would have mercy offered in the first place to the biggest sinners, because when they, any of them, receive it, it redounds most to the fame of his name.

Christ Jesus, as you may perceive, has put himself under the term of a physician, a doctor for curing of diseases: and you know that applause and fame, are things that physicians much desire. That is it that helps them to patients, and that also that will help their patients to commit themselves to their skill for cure, with the more confidence and repose of spirit. And the best way for a doctor or physician to get himself a name, is, in the first place, to take in hand, and cure some such as all others have given off for lost and dead. Physicians get neither name nor fame by pricking of wheals, or pricking out thistles, or by laying of plaisters to the scratch of a pin; every old woman can do this. But if they would have a name and a fame, if they will have it quickly they must, as I said, do some great and desperate cures. Let them fetch one to life that was dead; let them recover one to his wits that was mad; let them make one that was born blind to see; or let them give ripe wits to a fool; these are notable cures, and he that can do thus, and if he doth thus first, he shall have the name and fame he desires; he may lie a-bed till noon.

Why, Christ Jesus forgiveth sins for a name, and so begets of himself a good report in the hearts of the children of men. And therefore in reason he must be willing, as also he did command, that his mercy should be offered first to the biggest sinners.

"I will forgive their sins, iniquities, and transgressions," says he, "and it shall turn to me for a name of joy, and a praise and an honour, before all the nations of the earth;" Jer. xxxiii. 8, 9.

And hence it is, that at his first appearing he took upon him to do such mighty works: he got a fame thereby, he got a name thereby; Matt. iv. 23, 24.

When Christ had cast the legion of devils out of the man of

whom you read, Mark v., he bid him go home to his friends, and tell it: "Go home," saith he, "to thy friends, and tell them how great things God has done for thee, and has had compassion on thee;" Mark v. 19. Christ Jesus seeks a name, and desireth a fame in the world; and therefore, or the better to obtain that, he commands that mercy should first be proffered to the biggest sinners, because, by the saving of one of them he makes all men marvel. As 'tis said of the man last mentioned, whom Christ cured towards the beginning of his ministry: "And he departed," says the text, "and began to publish in Decapolis, how great things Jesus had done for him; and all men did marvel," ver. 20.

When John told Christ, that they saw one casting out devils in his name, and they forbade him, because he followed not with them, what is the answer of Christ? "Forbid him not: for there is no man which shall do a miracle in my name, that can lightly speak evil of me." No; they will rather cause his praise to be heard, and his name to be magnified, and so put glory on the head of Christ.

But we will follow a little our metaphor: Christ, as I said, has put himself under the term of a physician; consequently he desireth that his fame, as to the salvation of sinners, may spread abroad, and that the world may see what he can do. And to this end, he has not only commanded, that the biggest sinners should have the first offer of his mercy, but has, as physicians do, put out his bills, and published his doings, that things may be read and talked of. Yea, he has moreover, in these his blessed bills, the holy scriptures I mean, inserted the very names of persons, the places of their abode, and the great cures that, by the means of his salvations, he has wrought upon them to this very end. Here is, Item, such a one, by my grace and redeeming blood, was made a monument of everlasting life; and such a one, by my perfect obedience, became an heir of glory. And then he produceth their names.

Item, I saved Lot from the guilt and damnation that he had procured to himself by his incest.

Item, I saved David from the vengeance that belonged to him for committing of adultery and murder.

Here is also Solomon, Manasseh, Peter, Magdalen, and many others, made mention of in this book. Yea, here are their names, their sins, and their salvations recorded together, that you may read and know what a Saviour he is, and do him honour in the world. For why are these things thus recorded, but to show to sinners what he can do, to the praise and glory of his grace?

And it is observable, as I said before, we have but very little of the salvation of little sinners mentioned in God's book, because that would not have answered the design, to wit, to bring glory and fame to the name of the Son of God.

What should be the reason, think you, why Christ should so easily take a denial of the great ones, that were the grandeur of the world, and struggle so hard for hedge-creepers and highwaymen (as that parable, Luke xiv., seems to import he doth), but to show forth the riches of the glory of his grace to his praise? This I say, is one reason to be sure.

They that had their grounds, their yoke of oxen, and their marriage joys, were invited to come; but they made their excuse, and that served the turn. But when he comes to deal with the worst, he saith to his servants, Go ye out and bring them in hither. "Go out quickly, and bring in hither the poor, the maimed, the halt, and the blind." And they did so: and he said again, "Go out into the highways and hedges, and compel them to come in, that my house may be filled;" Luke xiv. 18, 19, 23. These poor, lame, maimed, blind, hedge-creepers and highwaymen, must come in, must be forced in. These, if saved, will make his merits shine.

When Christ was crucified, and hanged up between the earth and heavens, there were two thieves crucified with him; and behold, he lays hold of one of them and will have him away with him to glory. Was not this a strange act, and a display of unthought of grace? Were there none but thieves there, or were the rest of that company out of his reach? Could he not, think you, have stooped from the cross to the ground, and have laid hold on some honester man if he would? Yes, doubtless. Oh! but then he would not have displayed his grace, nor so have pursued his own designs, namely, to get to himself a praise and a name: but now he has done it to purpose. For who that shall read this story, but must confess, that the Son of God is full of grace; for a proof of the riches thereof, he left behind him, when upon the cross he took the thief away with him to glory. Nor can this one act of his be buried; it will be talked of to the end of the world to his praise. "Men shall speak of the might of thy terrible acts, and will declare thy greatness; they shall abundantly utter the memory of thy great goodness, and shall sing of thy righteousness. They shall speak of the glory of thy kingdom, and talk of thy power; to make known to the sons of men his mighty acts, and the glorious majesty of his kingdom;" Psalm cxlv. 6–12.

When the word of God came among the conjurers and those soothsayers that you read of, Acts xix., and had prevailed with some of them to accept of the grace of Christ, the Holy Ghost records it with a boast, for that it would redound to his praise, saying, "And many of them that used curious arts, brought their books together, and burned them before all men: and counted the price of them, and found it fifty thousand pieces of silver. So mightily grew the word of God, and prevailed;" Acts xix. 19, 20. It wrenched out of the clutches of Satan some of those of whom he thought himself most sure.

"So mightily grew the word of God." It grew mightily, it encroached upon the kingdom of the devil. It pursued him, and took the prey; it forced him to let go his hold: it brought away captive, as prisoners taken by force of arms, some of the most valiant of his army: it fetched back from, as it were, the confines of hell, some of those that were his most trusty, and that with hell had been at an agreement: it made them come and confess their deeds, and burn their books before all men: "So mightily grew the word of God, and prevailed."

Thus, therefore, you see why Christ will have mercy offered in the first place to the biggest sinners; they have most need thereof; and this is the most ready way to extol his name that rideth upon the heavens to our help. But,

Thirdly, Christ Jesus would have mercy offered in the first place to the biggest sinners, because by their forgiveness and salvation, others hearing of it, will be encouraged the more to come to him for life.

For the physician, by curing the most desperate at the first, doth not only get himself a name, but begets encouragement in the minds of other diseased folk to come to him for help. Hence you read of our Lord, that after, through his tender mercy, he had cured many of great diseases, his fame was spread abroad, "They brought unto him all sick people that were taken with divers diseases and torments, and those which were possessed with devils, and those which were lunatic, and those that had the palsy, and he healed them. And there followed him great multitudes of people from Galilee, and Decapolis, and Jerusalem, and Judea, and from beyond Jordan;" Matt. iv. 24, 25.

See here, he first by working gets himself a fame, a name, and renown, and now men take encouragement, and bring from all quarters their diseased to him, being helped, by what they had heard, to believe that their diseased should be healed.

Now, as he did with those outward cures, so he does in the proffers of his grace and mercy: he proffers that in the first place to the biggest sinners, that others may take heart to come to him to be saved. I will give you a scripture or two, I mean to show you that Christ, by commanding that his mercy should in the first place be offered to the biggest of sinners, has a design thereby to encourage and provoke others to come also to him for mercy.

"God," saith Paul, "who is rich in mercy, for his great love wherewith he loved us, even when we were dead in sins, hath quickened us together with Christ (by grace ye are saved); and hath raised us up together, and made us sit together in heavenly places in Christ Jesus." But why did he do all this? "That in the ages to come he might shew the exceeding riches of his grace in his kindness towards us through Christ Jesus;" Eph. ii. 4–7.

See, here is a design; God lets out his mercy to Ephesus of design, even to shew to the ages to come the exceeding riches of his grace, in his kindness to them through Christ Jesus. And why to shew by these the exceeding riches of his grace to the ages to come, through Christ Jesus, but to allure them, and their children also, to come to him, and to partake of the same grace through Christ Jesus?

But what was Paul, and the Ephesian sinners? (of Paul we will speak anon). These Ephesian sinners, they were men dead in sins, men that walked according to the dictates and motions of the devil; worshippers of Diana, that effeminate goddess; men far off from God, aliens and strangers to all good things; such as were far off from that, as I said, and consequently in a most deplorable condition. As the Jerusalem sinners were of the highest sort among the Jews, so these Ephesian sinners were of the highest sort among the Gentiles; Eph. ii. 1–3, 11, 12; Acts xix. 35.

Wherefore as by the Jerusalem sinners, in saving them first, he had a design to provoke others to come to him for mercy, so the same design is here set on foot again, in his calling and converting the Ephesian sinners, "That in the ages to come he might shew the exceeding riches of his grace," says he, "in his kindness towards us through Christ Jesus." There is yet one hint behind. It is said that God saved these for his love; that is, as I think, for the setting forth, for the commendations of his love, for the advance of his love, in the hearts and minds of them that should come after. As who should say, God has had mercy upon, and been gracious to you, that he might shew to others, for their encouragement, that they have ground to come to him to be saved. When God saves one great sinner, it is to encourage another great sinner to come to him for mercy.

He saved the thief, to encourage thieves to come to him for mercy; he saved Magdalen, to encourage other Magdalens to come to him for mercy; he saved Saul, to encourage Sauls to come to him for mercy; and this Paul himself doth say, "For this cause," saith he, "I obtained mercy, that in me first Jesus Christ might shew forth all long-suffering for a pattern to them which should hereafter believe on him to life everlasting;" 1 Tim. i. 16.

How plain are the words! Christ, in saving of me, has given to the world a pattern of his grace, that they might see and believe, and come, and be saved; that they that are to be born hereafter might believe on Jesus Christ to life everlasting.

But what was Paul? Why, he tells you himself; I am, says he, the chief of sinners: I was, says he, a blaspheme; a persecutor, an injurious person; but I obtained mercy; 1 Tim. i. 14, 15. Ay, that is well for you, Paul; but what advantage have we thereby? Oh, very much, saith he; for, "for this cause I obtained mercy, that in me first, Jesus Christ might shew all long-suffering for a pattern to them which shall believe on him to life everlasting."

Thus, therefore, you see that this third reason is of strength, namely, that Jesus Christ would have mercy offered in the first place to the biggest sinners, because, by their forgiveness and salvation, others, hearing of it, will be encouraged the more to come to him for mercy.

It may well therefore be said to God, Thou delightest in mercy, and mercy pleases thee; Mich. vii. 18.

But who believes that this was God's design in shewing mercy of old—namely, that we that come after might take courage to come to him for mercy; or that Jesus Christ would have mercy offered in the first place to the biggest sinners, to stir up others to come to him for life? This is not the manner of men, O God!

But David saw this betimes; therefore he makes this one argument with God, that he would blot out his transgressions, that he would forgive his adultery, his murders, and horrible hypocrisy. Do it, O Lord, saith he, do it, and "then will I teach transgressors thy ways, and sinners shall be converted unto thee;" Psalm li. 7–13.

He knew that the conversion of sinners would be a work highly pleasing to God, as being that which he had designed before he made mountain or hill: wherefore he comes, and he saith, Save me, O Lord; if thou wilt but save me, I will fall in with thy design; I will help to bring what sinners to thee I can. And, Lord, I am willing to be made a preacher myself; for that I have been a horrible sinner: wherefore, if thou shalt forgive my great transgressions, I shall be a fit man to tell of thy wondrous grace to others. Yea, Lord, I dare promise, that if thou wilt have mercy upon me, it shall tend to the glory of thy grace, and also to the increase of thy kingdom; for I will tell it, and sinners will hear on't. And there is nothing so suiteth with the hearing sinner as mercy, and to be informed that God is willing to bestow it upon him. "I will teach transgressors thy ways, and sinners shall be converted unto thee."

Nor will Christ Jesus miss of his design in proffering of mercy in the first place to the biggest sinners. You know what work the

Lord, by laying hold of the woman of Samaria, made among the people there. They knew that she was a town sinner, an adulteress, yea, one that after the most audacious manner lived in uncleanness with a man that was not her husband: but when she, from a turn upon her heart, went into the city, and said to her neighbours, "Come," Oh how they came! how they flocked out of the city to Jesus Christ! "Then they went out of the city, and came to him." "And many of the Samaritans (people perhaps as bad as herself) believed on him, for the saying of the woman, which testified, saying, he told me all that ever I did;" John iv. 39.

That word, "He told me all that ever I did," was a great argument with them; for by that they gathered, that though he knew her to be vile, yet he did not despise her, nor refuse to shew how willing he was to communicate his grace unto her; and this fetched over, first her, then them.

This woman, as I said, was a Samaritan sinner, a sinner of the worst complexion: for the Jews abhorred to have ought to do with them, ver. 9; wherefore none more fit than she to be made one of the decoys of heaven, to bring others of these Samaritan wild-fowls under the net of the grace of Christ. And she did the work to purpose. Many, and many more of the Samaritans believed on him; ver. 40–42. The heart of man, though set on sin, will, when it comes once to a persuasion that God is willing to have mercy upon us, incline to come to Jesus Christ for life.

Witness those turn-aways from God that you also read of in Jeremiah; for after they had heard three or four times over, that God had mercy for backsliders, they broke out, and said,

"Behold, we come unto thee, for thou art the Lord our God." Or as those in Hosea did, "For in thee the fatherless find mercy;" Jer. iii. 22; Hos. xiv. 1–3.

Mercy, and the revelation thereof, is the only antidote against sin. It is of a thawing nature; it will loose the heart that is frozen up in sin; yea, it will make the unwilling willing to come to Jesus Christ for life. Wherefore, do you think, was it that Jesus Christ told the adulterous woman, and that before so many sinners, that he had not condemned her, but to allure her, with them there present, to hope to find favour at his hands? (As he also saith in another place, "I came not to judge, but to save the world.") For might they not thence most rationally conclude, that if Jesus Christ had rather save than damn an harlot, there was encouragement for them to come to him for mercy.

I heard once a story from a soldier, who with his company had laid siege against a fort, that so long as the besieged were persuaded their foes would shew them no favour, they fought like madmen; but when they saw one of their fellows taken, and received to favour, they all came tumbling down from their fortress, and delivered themselves into their enemies' hands.

I am persuaded, did men believe that there is that grace and willingness in the heart of Christ to save sinners, as the word imports there is, they would come tumbling into his arms: but Satan has blinded their minds, that they cannot see this thing. Howbeit, the Lord Jesus has, as I said, that others might take heart and come to him, given out a commandment, that mercy should in the first place be offered to the biggest sinners. "Begin," saith he, "at Jerusalem." And thus I end the third reason.

Fourthly, Jesus Christ would have mercy offered in the first place to the biggest sinners, because that is the way, if they receive it, most to weaken the kingdom of Satan, and to keep it lowest in every age of the world. The biggest sinners, they are Satan's colonels and captains, the leaders of his people, and they that most stoutly make head against the Son of God. Wherefore let these first be conquered, and his kingdom will be weak. When Ishbosheth had lost his Abner, his kingdom was made weak: nor did he sit but tottering then upon his throne. So when Satan loseth his strong men, them that are mighty to work iniquity, and dexterous to manage others in the same, then is his kingdom weak; 2 Sam. iii. Therefore, I say, Christ doth offer mercy in the first place to such, the more to weaken his kingdom. Christ Jesus was glad to see Satan fall like lightning from heaven, that is, suddenly or head long; and it was, surely, by casting of him out of strong possessions, and by recovering of some notorious sinners out of his clutches; Luke x. 17–19.

Samson, when he would pull down the Philistines temple, took hold of the two main pillars of it, and breaking them, down came the house. Christ came to destroy the works of the devil, and to destroy by converting grace, as well as by redeeming blood. Now sin swarms, and lieth by legions, and whole armies, in the souls of the biggest sinners, as in garrisons: wherefore the way, the most direct way to destroy it, is first to deal with such sinners by the word of his gospel, and by the merits of his passion.

For example, though I shall give you but a homely one: suppose a family to be troubled with vermin, and one or two of the family to be in chief the breeders, the way, the quickest way to clear that family, or at least to weaken the so swarming of those vermin, is, in the first place, to sweeten the skin, head, and clothes of the chief breeders; and then, though all the family should be apt to breed them, the number of them, and so the greatness of that plague there, will be the more impaired.

Why, there are some people that are in chief the devil's sin-breeders in the towns and places where they live. The place, town, or family where they live, must needs be horribly verminous, as it were, eaten up with vermin. Now, let the Lord Jesus, in the first place, cleanse these great breeders, and there will be given a nip to those swarms of sins that used to be committed in such places throughout the town, house, or family, where such sin-breeding persons used to be.

I speak by experience: I was one of these verminous ones, one of these great sin-breeders; I infected all the youth of the town where I was born, with all manner of youthful vanities. The neighbours counted me so; my practice proved me so: wherefore Christ Jesus took me first, and taking me first, the contagion was much allayed all the town over. When God made me sigh, they would hearken, and enquiringly say, What is the matter with John? They also gave their various opinions of me: but, as I said, sin cooled, and failed, as to his full career. When I went out to seek the bread of life, some of them would follow, and the rest be put into a muse at home. Yea, almost the town, at first, at times would go out to hear at the place where I found good; yea, young and old for a while had some reformation on them; also some of them, perceiving that God had mercy upon me, came crying to him for mercy too.

But what need I give you an instance of poor I; I will come to Manasseh the king. So long as he was a ring-leading sinner, the great idolater, the chief for devilism, the whole land flowed with wickedness; for he "made them to sin," and do worse than the heathen that dwelt round about them, or that was cast out from before them: but when God converted him, the whole land was reformed. Down went the groves, the idols, and altars of Baal, and up went true religion in much of the power and purity of it. You will say, The king reformed by power. I answer, doubtless, and by example too; for people observe their leaders; as their fathers did, so did they; 2 Chron. xxxiii. 2.

This, therefore, is another reason why Jesus would have mercy offered in the first place to the biggest sinners, because that is the best way, if they receive it, most to weaken the kingdom of Satan, and to keep it poor and low.

And do you not think now, that if God would but take hold of the hearts of some of the most notorious in your town, in your family, or country, that this thing would be verified before your faces? It would, it would, to the joy of you that are godly, to the making of hell to sigh, to the great suppressing of sin, the glory of Christ, and the joy of the angels of God. And ministers should, therefore, that this work might go on, take advantages to persuade with the biggest sinners to come into Christ, according to my text, and their commissions; "Beginning at Jerusalem."

Fifthly, Jesus Christ would have mercy offered, in the first place, to the biggest sinners; because such, when converted, are usually the best helps in the church against temptations, and fittest for the support of the feeble-minded there. Hence, usually, you have some such in the first plantation of churches, or quickly upon it. Churches would do but sorrily, if Christ Jesus did not put such converts among them: they are the monuments and mirrors of mercy. The very sight of such a sinner in God's house, yea, the very thought of him, where the sight of him cannot be had, is ofttimes greatly for the help of the faith of the feeble.

"When the churches (said Paul) that were in Judea, heard this concerning me, that he which persecuted them in time past, now preached the faith which once he destroyed, they glorified God in me;" Gal. i. 20–24.

"Glorified God." How is that? Why, they praised him, and took courage to believe the more in the mercy of God; for that he had had mercy on such a great sinner as he. They glorified God "in me;" they wondered that grace should be so rich, as to take hold of such a wretch as I was; and for my sake believed in Christ the more.

There are two things that great sinners are acquainted with, when they come to divulge them to the saints, that are a great relief to their faith.

1. The contests that they usually have with the devil at their parting with him.

2. Their knowledge of his secrets in his workings.

For the first, The biggest sinners have usually great contests with the devil at their partings; and this is an help to saints: for ordinary saints find afterwards what the vile ones find at first, but when at the opening of hearts, the one finds himself to be as the other, the one is a comfort to the other. The lesser sort of sinners find but little of this, till after they have been some time in profession; but the vile man meets with his at the beginning. Wherefore he, when the other is down, is ready to tell that he has met with the same before; for, I say, he has had it before. Satan is loath to part with a great sinner. What my true servant (quoth he), my old servant, wilt thou forsake me now? having so often sold thyself to me to work wickedness, wilt thou forsake me now? Thou horrible wretch, dost not know, that thou hast sinned thyself beyond the reach of grace, and dost think to find mercy now? Art not thou a murderer, a thief, a harlot, a witch, a sinner of the greatest size, and dost thou look for mercy now? Dost thou think that Christ will foul his fingers with thee?

'Tis enough to make angels blush, saith Satan, to see so vile a one knock at heaven-gates for mercy, and wilt thou be so abominably bold to do it? Thus Satan dealt with me, says the great sinner, when at first I came to Jesus Christ. And what did you reply? saith the tempted. Why, I granted the whole charge to be true, says the other. And what, did you despair, or how? No, saith he, I said, I am Magdalen, I am Zaccheus, I am the thief, I am the harlot, I am the publican, I am the prodigal, and one of Christ's murderers: yea, worse than any of these; and yet God was so far off from rejecting of me (as I found afterwards), that there was music and dancing in his house for me, and for joy that I was come home unto him. O blessed be God for grace (says the other), for then I hope there is favour for me. Yea, as I told you, such a one is a continual spectacle in the church, for every one to behold God's grace and wonder by.

Secondly, And as for the secrets of Satan, such as are suggestions to question the being of God, the truth of his word, and to be annoyed with devilish blasphemies; none more acquainted with these than the biggest sinners at their conversion; wherefore thus also they are prepared to be helps in the church to relieve and comfort the other.

I might also here tell you of the contests and battles that such are engaged in, wherein they find the besettings of Satan, above any other of the saints. At which times Satan assaults the soul with darkness, fears, frightful thoughts of apparitions; now they sweat, pant, cry out, and struggle for life.

The angels now come down to behold the sight, and rejoice to see a bit of dust and ashes to overcome principalities and powers, and might, and dominions. But, as I said when these come a little to be settled, they are prepared for helping others, and are great comforts unto them. Their great sins give great encouragement to the devil to assault them; and by these temptations Christ takes advantage to make them the more helpful to the churches.

The biggest sinner, when he is converted, and comes into the church, says to them all, by his very coming in, Behold me, all you that are men and women of a low and timorous spirit, you whose hearts are narrow, for that you never had the advantage to know, because your sins are few, the largeness of the grace of God. Behold, I say, in me, the exceeding riches of his grace! I am a pattern set forth before your faces, on whom you may look and take heart. This, I say, the great sinner can say, to the exceeding comfort of all the rest.

Wherefore, as I have hinted before, when God intends to stock a place with saints, and to make that place excellently to flourish with the riches of his grace, he usually begins with the conversion of some of the most notorious thereabouts, and lays them as an example to allure others, and to build up when they are converted.

It was Paul that must go to the Gentiles, because Paul was the most outrageous of all the apostles, in the time of his unregeneracy. Yea, Peter must be he, that after his horrible fall, was thought fittest, when recovered again, to comfort and strengthen his brethren. See Luke xxii. 31, 32.

Some must be pillars in God's house; and if they be pillars of cedar, they must stand while they are stout and sturdy sticks in the forest, before they are cut down, and planted or placed there.

No man, when he buildeth his house, makes the principal parts thereof of weak or feeble timber; for how could such bear up the rest? but of great and able wood. Christ Jesus also goeth this way to work; he makes of the biggest sinners bearers and supporters to the rest. This then, may serve for another reason, why Jesus Christ gives out in commandment, that mercy should, in the first place, be offered to the biggest sinners: because such, when converted, are usually the best helps in the church against temptations, and fittest for the support of the feeble-minded there.

Sixthly, Another reason why Jesus Christ would have mercy offered in the first place to the biggest sinners, is, because they, when converted, are apt to love him most.

This agrees both with Scripture and reason. Scripture says so: "To whom much is forgiven, the same loveth much. To whom little is forgiven, the same loveth little;" Luke vii. 47. Reason says so: for as it would be the unreasonablest thing in the world to render hatred for love, and contempt for forgiveness; so it would be as ridiculous to think, that the reception of a little kindness should lay the same obligations upon the heart to love, as the reception of a great deal. I would not disparage the love of Christ; I know the least drachm of it, when it reaches to forgiveness, is great above all the world; but comparatively, there are greater extensions of the love of Christ to one than to another. He that has most sin, if forgiven, is partaker of the greatest love, of the greatest forgiveness.

I know also, that there are some, that from this very doctrine say, "Let us do evil that good may come;" and that turn the grace of our God into lasciviousness. But I speak not of these; these will neither be ruled by grace nor reason. Grace would teach them, if they know it, to deny ungodly courses; and so would reason too, if it could truly sense the love of God; Titus ii. 11, 12; Rom. xi. 1.

Doth it look like what hath any coherence with reason or mercy, for a man to abuse his friend? Because Christ died for men, shall I therefore spit in his face? The bread and water that was given by Elisha to his enemies, that came into the land of Israel to take him, had so much influence upon their minds, though heathens, that they returned to their homes without hurting him: yea, it kept them from coming again in a hostile manner into the coasts of Israel; 2 Kings vi. 19–23.

But to forbear to illustrate till anon. One reason why Christ

Jesus shews mercy to sinners, is, that he might obtain their love, that he may remove their base affections from base objects to himself. Now, if he loves to be loved a little, he loves to be loved much; but there is not any that are capable of loving much, save those that have much forgiven them. Hence it is said of Paul, that he laboured more than them all; to wit, with a labour of love, because he had been by sin more vile against Christ than they all; 1 Cor. xv. He it was that persecuted the church of God, and wasted it; Gal. i. 13. He of them all was the only raving bedlam against the saints: "And being exceeding mad," says he, "against them, I persecuted them, even to strange cities;" Acts xxvi. 11.

This raving bedlam, that once was so, is he that now says, I laboured more than them all, more for Christ than them all.

But Paul, what moved thee thus to do? The love of Christ, says he. It was not I, but the grace of God that was with me. As who should say, O grace! It was such grace to save me! It was such marvellous grace for God to look down from heaven upon me, and that secured me from the wrath to come, that I am captivated with the sense of the riches of it. Hence I act, hence I labour; for how can I otherwise do, since God not only separated me from my sins and companions, but separated all the powers of my soul and body to his service? I am therefore prompted on by this exceeding love to labour as I have done; yet not I, but the grace of God with me.

Oh! I shall never forget his love, nor the circumstances under which I was, when his love laid hold upon me. I was going to Damascus with letters from the high-priest, to make havock of

God's people there, as I had made havock of them in other places. These bloody letters were not imposed upon me. I went to the high-priest and desired them of him; Acts ix. 1, 2; and yet he saved me! I was one of the men, of the chief men, that had a hand in the blood of his martyr Stephen; yet he had mercy on me! When I was at Damascus, I stunk so horribly like a blood-sucker, that I became a terror to all thereabout. Yea, Ananias (good man) made intercession to my Lord against me; yet he would have mercy upon me, yea, joined mercy to mercy, until he had made me a monument of grace! He made a saint of me, and persuaded me that my transgressions were forgiven me.

When I began to preach, those that heard me were amazed, and said, "Is not this he that destroyed them that called on this name in Jerusalem, and came hither for that intent, that he might bring them bound to the high-priest?" Hell doth know that I was a sinner; heaven doth know that I was a sinner; the world also knows that I was a sinner, a sinner of the greatest size; but I obtained mercy; 1 Tim i. 15, 16.

Shall not this lay obligation upon me? Is not love of the greatest force to oblige? Is it not strong as death, cruel as the grave, and hotter than the coals of juniper? Hath it not a most vehement flame? can the waters quench it? can the floods drown it? I am under the force of it, and this is my continual cry, What shall I render to the Lord for all the benefits which he has bestowed upon me?

Ay, Paul! this is something; thou speakest like a man, like a man affected, and carried away with the love and grace of God. Now, this sense, and this affection, and this labour, giveth to

Christ the love that he looks for. But he might have converted twenty little sinners, and yet not found, for grace bestowed, so much love in them all.

I wonder how far a man might go among the converted sinners of the smaller size, before one could find one that so much as looked any thing this wayward. Where is he that is thus under pangs of love for the grace bestowed upon him by Jesus Christ? Excepting only some few, you may walk to the world's end, and find none. But, as I said, some there are, and so there has been in every age of the church, great sinners, that have had much forgiven them; and they love much upon this account.

Jesus Christ therefore knows what he doth, when he lays hold on the hearts of sinners of the biggest size. He knows that such an one will love more than many that have not sinned half their sins.

I will tell you a story that I have read of Martha and Mary; the name of the book I have forgot; I mean of the book in which I found the relation; but the thing was thus: Martha, saith my author, was a very holy woman, much like Lazarus her brother; but Mary was a loose and wanton creature; Martha did seldom miss good sermons and lectures, when she could come at them in Jerusalem; but Mary would frequent the house of sports, and the company of the vilest of men for lust: And though Martha had often desired that her sister would go with her to hear her preachers, yea, had often entreated her with tears to do it, yet could she never prevail; for still Mary would make her excuse, or reject her with disdain for her zeal and preciseness in religion.

After Martha had waited long, tried many ways to bring her

sister to good, and all proved ineffectual, at last she comes upon her thus: "Sister," quoth she, "I pray thee go with me to the temple to-day, to hear one preach a sermon." "What kind of preacher is he?" said she. Martha replied, "It is one Jesus of Nazareth; he is the handsomest man that ever you saw with your eyes. Oh! he shines in beauty, and is a most excellent preacher."

Now, what does Mary, after a little pause, but goes up into her chamber, and with her pins and her clouts, decks up herself as fine as her fingers could make her.

This done, away she goes, not with her sister Martha, but as much unobserved as she could, to the sermon, or rather to see the preacher.

The hour and preacher being come, and she having observed whereabout the preacher would stand, goes and sets herself so in the temple, that she might be sure to have the full view of this excellent person. So he comes in, and she looks, and the first glimpse of his person pleased her. Well, Jesus addresseth himself to his sermon, and she looks earnestly on him.

Now, at that time, saith my author, Jesus preached about the lost sheep, the lost groat, and the prodigal child. And when he came to shew what care the shepherd took for one lost sheep, and how the woman swept to find her piece which was lost, and what joy there was at their finding, she began to be taken by the ears, and forgot what she came about, musing what the preacher would make of it. But when he came to the application, and shewed, that by the lost sheep was meant a great sinner; by the shepherd's care, was meant God's love for great sinners; and that by the joy of the neighbours, was shewed what joy there was among the angels in heaven over one great sinner that repenteth; she began to be taken by the heart. And as he spake these last words, she thought he pitched his innocent eyes just upon her, and looked as if he spake what was now said to her: wherefore her heart began to tremble, being shaken with affection and fear; then her eyes ran down with tears apace; wherefore she was forced to hide her face with her handkerchief; and so sat sobbing and crying all the rest of the sermon.

Sermon being done, up she gets, and away she goes, and withal inquired where this Jesus the preacher dined that day? and one told her, At the house of Simon the Pharisee. So away goes she, first to her chamber, and there strips herself of her wanton attire: then falls upon her knees to ask God forgiveness for all her wicked life. This done, in a modest dress she goes to Simon's house, where she finds Jesus sat at dinner. So she gets behind him, and weeps, and drops her tears upon his feet like rain, and washes them, and wipes them with the hair of her head. She also kissed his feet with her lips, and anointed them with ointment. When Simon the Pharisee perceived what the woman did, and being ignorant of what it was to be forgiven much (for he never was forgiven more than fifty pence), he began to think within himself, that he had been mistaken about Jesus Christ, because he suffered such a sinner as this woman was, to touch him. Surely, quoth he, this man, if he were a prophet, would not let this woman come near him, for she is a town-sinner (so ignorant are all self-righteous men of the way of Christ with sinners.) But lest Mary should be discouraged with some clownish carriage of this Pharisee and so desert her good beginnings, and her new steps which she now had begun to take towards eternal life, Jesus began thus with Simon. "Simon," saith he, "I have somewhat to say unto thee. And he saith, Master, say on. There was," said Jesus, "a certain creditor had two debtors; the one owed five hundred pence, and the other fifty. And when they had nothing to pay, he frankly forgave them both. Tell me therefore which of them will love him most? Simon answered and said, I suppose that he to whom he forgave most. And he said unto him, Thou hast rightly judged. And he turned to the woman, and said unto Simon, Seest thou this woman? I entered into thy house, thou gavest me no water for my feet; but she hath washed my feet with tears, and wiped them with the hairs of her head. Thou gavest me no kiss: but this woman, since the time I came in, hath not ceased to kiss my feet. My head with oil thou didst not anoint, but this woman hath anointed my feet with ointment. Wherefore I say unto thee, Her sins which are many, are forgiven, for she loved much; but to whom little is forgiven, the same loveth little. And he said unto her, Thy sins are forgiven;" Luke vii. 36–50.

Thus you have the story. If I come short in any circumstance, I beg pardon of those that can correct me. It is three or four and twenty years since I saw the book: yet I have, as far as my memory will admit, given you the relation of the matter. However Luke, as you see, doth here present you with the substance of the whole.

Alas! Christ Jesus has but little thanks for the saving of little sinners. "To whom little is forgiven, the same loveth little." He gets not water for his feet, by his saving of such sinners. There are abundance of dry-eyed Christians in the world, and abundance of dry-eyed duties too; duties that never were wetted with the tears of contrition and repentance, nor ever sweetened with the great sinner's box of ointment. And the reason is, such sinners have not great sins to be saved from; or if they have, they look upon them in the diminishing glass of the holy law of God. But I rather believe, that the professors of our days want a due sense of what they are; for, verily, for the generality of them, both before and since conversion, they have been sinners of a lusty size. But if their eyes be holden, if convictions are not shewn, if their knowledge of their sins is but like to the eye-sight in twilight; the heart cannot be affected with that grace that has laid hold on the man; and so Christ Jesus sows much, and has little coming in.

Wherefore his way is ofttimes to step out of the way, to Jericho, to Samaria, to the country of the Gadarenes, to the coasts of Tyre and Sidon, and also to Mount Calvary, that he may lay hold of such kind of sinners as will love him to his liking; Luke xix. 1–11; John iv. 3–11; Mark v. 1–21; Matt. xv. 21–29; Luke xxiii. 33–44.

But thus much for the sixth reason, why Christ Jesus would have mercy offered in the first place to the biggest sinners, to wit, because such sinners, when converted, are apt to love him most. The Jerusalem sinners were they that outstripped, when they were converted, in some things, all the churches of the Gentiles. "They were of one heart, and of one soul, neither said any of them, that aught of the things that they possessed was their own." "Neither was there any among them that lacked: for as many as were possessors of lands or houses sold them, and brought the price of the things that were sold, and laid them down at the apostles' feet," &c.; Acts iv. 32–35. Now, shew me such another pattern if you can. But why did these do thus? Oh! they were Jerusalem sinners. These were the men that but a little before had killed the Prince of Life; and those to whom he did, that notwithstanding, send the first offer of grace and mercy. And the sense of this took them up betwixt the earth and the heaven, and carried them on in such ways and methods as could never be trodden by any since. They talk of the church of Rome, and set her in her primitive state, as a pattern and mother of churches; when the truth is, they were the Jerusalem sinners, when converts, that out-did all the churches that ever were.

Seventhly, Christ Jesus would have mercy offered, in the first place, to the biggest sinners; because grace when it is received by such, finds matter to kindle upon more freely than it finds in other sinners. Great sinners are like the dry wood, or like great candles, which burn best and shine with biggest light. I lay not this down, as I did those reasons before, to shew, that when great sinners are converted, they will be encouragement to others, though that is true; but to shew that Christ has a delight to see grace, the grace we receive, to shine. We love to see things that bear a good gloss; yea, we choose to buy such kind of matter to work upon, as will, if wrought up to what we intend, cast that lustre that we desire.

Candles that burn not bright, we like not: wood that is green will rather smother, and sputter, and smoke, and crack, and flounce, than cast a brave light and a pleasant heat: wherefore great folks care not much, not so much for such kind of things, as for them that will better answer their ends.

Hence Christ desires the biggest sinner; in him there is matter to work by, to wit, a great deal of sin; for as by the tallow of the candle, the fire takes occasion to burn the brighter; so by the sin of the soul, grace takes occasion to shine the clearer. Little candles shine but little, for there wanteth matter for the fire to work upon; but in the great sinner, here is more matter for grace to work by. Faith shines, when it worketh towards Christ, through the sides of many and great transgressors, and so does love, for that much is forgiven. And what matter can be found in the soul for humility to work by so well, as by a sight that I have been and am an abominable sinner? And the same is to be said of patience, meekness, gentleness, self-denial, or of any other grace. Grace takes occasion by the vileness of the man to shine the more; even as by the ruggedness of a very strong distemper or disease, the virtue of the medicine is best made manifest. Where sin abounds, grace much more abounds; Rom. v. 20. A black string makes the neck look whiter; great sins make grace burn clear. Some say, when grace and a good nature meet together, they do make shining Christians: but I say, when grace and a great sinner meet, and when grace shall subdue that great sinner to itself, and shall operate after its kind in the soul of that great sinner, then we have a shining Christian; witness all those of whom mention was made before.

Abraham was among the idolaters when in the land of Assyria, and served idols with his kindred on the other side of the flood; Jos. xxiv. 2; Gen. xi. 31. But who, when called, was there in the world, in whom grace shone so bright as in him?

The Thessalonians were idolaters before the word of God came to them; but when they had received it, they became examples to all that did believe in Macedonia and Achaia; 1 Thess. i. 6–10.

God the Father, and Jesus Christ his Son, are for having things seen, for having the word of life held forth. They light not a candle that it might be put under a bushel, or under a bed, but on a candlestick, that all that come in may see the light; Matt. v. 15; Mark iv. 21; Luke viii. 16; chap. xi. 33.

And, I say, as I said before, in whom is light like so to shine, as in the souls of great sinners?

When the Jewish Pharisees dallied with the gospel, Christ threatened to take it from them, and to give it to the barbarous heathens and idolaters. Why so? For they, saith he, will bring forth the fruits thereof in their season: "Therefore say I unto you, The kingdom of God shall be taken from you, and given to a nation bringing forth the fruits thereof;" Matt. xxi. 41–43.

I have often marvelled at our youth, and said in my heart, What should be the reason that they should be so generally at this day debauched as they are? For they are now profane to amazement; and sometimes I have thought one thing, and sometimes another; that is, why God should suffer it so to be. At last I have thought of this: How if the God, whose ways are past finding out, should suffer it so to be now, that he might make of some of them the more glorious saints hereafter. I know sin is of the devil, but it cannot work in the world without permission: and if it happens to be as I have thought, it will not be the first time that God the Lord hath caught Satan in his own design. For my part, I believe that the time is at hand, that we shall see better saints in the world than has been seen in it this many a day. And this vileness, that at present does so much swallow up our youth, is one cause of my thinking so: for out of them, for from among them, when God sets to his hand, as of old, you shall see what penitent ones, what trembling ones, and what admirers of grace, will be found to profess the gospel to the glory of God by Christ.

Alas! we are a company of worn-out Christians, our moon is in the wane; we are much more black than white, more dark than light; we shine but a little; grace in the most of us is decayed. But I say, when they of these debauched ones that are to be saved shall be brought in, when these that look more like devils than men shall be converted to Christ (and I believe several of them will), then will Christ be exalted, grace adored, the word prized, Zion's path better trodden, and men in the pursuit of their own salvation, to the amazement of them that are left behind.

Just before Christ came into the flesh, the world was degenerated as it is now: the generality of the men in Jerusalem, were become either high and famous for hypocrisy, or filthy base in their lives. The devil also was broke loose in a hideous manner, and had taken possession of many: yea, I believe that there was never generation before nor since, that could produce so many possessed with devils, deformed, lame, blind, and infected with monstrous diseases, as that generation could. But what was the reason thereof, I mean the reason from God? Why one (and we may sum up more in that answer that Christ gave to his disciples concerning him that was born blind) was, that the works of God might be made manifest in them, and that the Son of God might be glorified thereby, John ix. 2, 3; chap. xi. 4.

Now if these devils and diseases, as they possessed men then, were to make way and work for an approaching Christ in person, and for the declaring of his power, why may we not think that now, even now also, he is ready to come by his Spirit in the gospel to heal many of the debaucheries of our age? I cannot believe that grace will take them all, for there are but few that are saved; but yet it will take some, even some of the worst of men, and make blessed ones of them. But, O how these ringleaders in vice will then shine in virtue! They will be the very pillars in churches, they will be as an ensign in the land. "The Lord their God shall save them in that day as the flock of his people: for they shall be as the stones of a crown, lifted up as an ensign upon his land;" Zech. ix. 16. But who are these? Even idolatrous Ephraim, and backsliding Judah; ver. 13.

I know there is ground to fear, that the iniquity of this generation will be pursued with heavy judgments: but that will not hinder what we have supposed. God took him a glorious church out of bloody Jerusalem, yea, out of the chief of the sinners there, and left the rest to be taken and spoiled, and sold, thirty for a penny, in the nations where they were captives. The gospel working gloriously in a place, to the seizing upon many of the ringleading sinners thereof, promiseth no security to the rest, but rather threateneth them with the heaviest and smartest judgments; as in the instance now given, we have a full demonstration; but in defending, the Lord will defend his people; and in saving, he will save his inheritance.

Nor does this speak any great comfort to a decayed and backsliding sort of Christians; for the next time God rides post with his gospel, he will leave such Christians behind him. But I say, Christ is resolved to set up his light in the world; yea, he is delighted to see his graces shine; and therefore he commands that his gospel should to that end be offered, in the first place, to the biggest sinners; for by great sins it shineth most; therefore he saith, "Begin at Jerusalem."

Eighthly, and lastly, Christ Jesus will have mercy to be offered in the first place to the biggest sinners; for that by that means the impenitent that are left behind will be at the judgment the more left without excuse.

God's word has two edges; it can cut back-stroke and fore-stroke: if it doth thee no good, it will do thee hurt; it is the savour of life unto life to those that receive it, but of death unto death to them that refuse it; 2 Cor. ii. 15, 16. But this is not all; the tender of grace to the biggest sinners in the first place, will not only leave the rest, or those that refuse it, in a deplorable condition, but will also stop their mouths, and cut off all pretence to excuse at that day. "If I had not come and spoken unto them," saith Christ, "they had not had sin; but now they have no cloak for their sin," for their sin of persevering in impenitence; Job xv. 22.

But what did he speak to them? Why, even that which I have told you; to wit, That he has in special a delight in saving the biggest sinners. He spake this in the way of his doctrine; he spake this in the way of his practice, even to the pouring out of his last breath before them; Luke xxiii. 34.

Now, since this is so, what can the condemned at the judgment say for themselves, why sentence of death should not be passed upon them? I say, what excuse can they make for themselves, when they shall be asked why they did not in the day of salvation come to Christ to be saved? Will they have ground to say to the Lord, Thou wast only for saving of little sinners; and therefore because they were great ones, they durst not come unto him? or that thou hadst not compassion for the biggest sinners, therefore I died in despair? Will these be excuses for them, as the case now standeth with them? Is there not every where in God's book a flat contradiction to this, in multitudes of promises, of invitations, of examples, and the like? Alas, alas! there will then be there millions of souls to confute this plea; ready, I say, to stand up, and say, O! deceived world, heaven swarms with such, as were, when they were in the world, to the full as bad as you.

Now, this will kill all plea or excuse, why they should perish in their sins; yea, the text says, they shall see them there. "There shall be weeping, when you shall see Abraham, and Isaac, and Jacob, and all the prophets in the kingdom of heaven, and you yourselves thrust out. And they shall come from the east, and from the west, and from the north, and from the south, and shall sit down in the kingdom of God;" Luke xiii. 28, 29. Out of which company it is easy to pick such as sometimes were as bad people as any that now breathe on the face of the earth. What think you of the first man, by whose sins there are millions now in hell? And so I may say, What think you of ten thousand more besides?

But if the world will not stifle and gag them up (I speak now for amplification's sake), the view of those who are saved shall.

There comes an incestuous person to the bar, and pleads, That the bigness of his sins was a bar to his receiving the promise. But will not his mouth be stopped as to that, when Lot and the incestuous Corinthian shall be set before him; Gen. xix. 33–37; 1 Cor. v. 1, 2.

There comes a thief, and says, Lord, my sin of theft, I thought, was such as could not be pardoned by thee! But when he shall see the thief that was saved on the cross stand by, as clothed with beauteous glory, what further can he be able to object? Yea, the Lord will produce ten thousand of his saints at his coming, who shall after this manner execute judgment upon all, and so convince all that are ungodly among them, of all their hard speeches which ungodly sinners have spoken against him. And these are hard speeches against him, to say that he was not able or willing to save men, because of the greatness of their sins, or to say that they were discouraged by his word from repentance, because of the heinousness of their offences.

These things, I say, shall then be confuted: he comes with ten thousand of his saints to confute them, and to stop their mouths from making objections against their own eternal damnation.

Here is Adam, the destroyer of the world; here is Lot, that lay with both his daughters; here is Abraham, that was sometime an idolater, and Jacob, that was a supplanter, and Reuben, that lay with his father's concubine, and Judah that lay with his daughter-in-law, and Levi and Simeon that wickedly slew thee Shechemites, and Aaron that great backslider, and Manassah that man of blood and that made an idol to be worshipped, and that proclaimed a religious feast unto it. Here is also Rachab the harlot, and Bathsheba that bare a bastard to David. Here is Solomon a witch. Time would fail me to tell you of the woman of Canaan's daughter, Magdalen, of Matthew the publican, and of Gideon and Sampson, and many thousands more.

Alas! alas! I say, what will these sinners do, that have, through their unbelief, eclipsed the glorious largeness of the mercy of God, and gave way to despair of salvation, because of the bigness of their sins?

For all these, though now glorious saints in light, were sometimes sinners of the biggest size, who had sins that were of a notorious hue; yet now, I say, they are in their shining and heavenly robes before the throne of God and of the Lamb, blessing for ever and ever that Son of God for their salvation, who died for them upon the tree; admiring that ever it should come into their hearts once to think of coming to God by Christ; but above all, blessing God for granting of them light to see those encouragements in his testament; without which, without doubt, they had been daunted and sunk down under guilt of sin and despair, as their fellow-sinners have done.

But now they also are witnesses for God, and for his grace against an unbelieving world; for, as I said, they shall come to convince the world of their speeches, their hard and unbelieving words, that they have spoken concerning the mercy of God, and the merits of the passion of his blessed Son Jesus Christ.

But will it not, think you, strangely put to silence all such thoughts, and words, and reasonings of the ungodly before the bar of God? Doubtless it will; yea and will send them away from his presence also, with the greatest guilt that possibly can fasten upon the consciences of men.

For what will sting like this?—I have, through mine own foolish, narrow, unworthy, undervaluing thoughts, of the love and ability of Christ to save me, brought myself to everlasting ruin.

It is true, I was a horrible sinner; not one in a hundred did live so vile a life as I: but this should not have kept me from closing with Jesus Christ: I see now that there are abundance in glory that once were as bad as I have been: but they were saved by faith, and I am damned by unbelief.

Wretch that I am! why did not I give glory to the redeeming blood of Jesus? Why did I not humbly cast my soul at his blessed footstool for mercy? Why did I judge of his ability to save me by the voice of my shallow reason, and the voice of a guilty conscience? Why betook not I myself to the holy word of God? Why did I not read and pray that I might understand, since now I perceive that God said then, he giveth liberally to them that pray, and upbraideth not; Jam. i. 5.

It is rational to think, that by such cogitations as these the unbelieving world will be torn in pieces before the judgment of Christ; especially those that have lived where they did or might have heard the gospel of the grace of God. Oh! that saying, "It shall be more tolerable for Sodom at the judgment than for them," will be better understood. See Luke x. 8–12.

This reason, therefore, standeth fast; namely, that Christ, by offering mercy in the first place to the biggest sinner now, will stop all mouths of the impenitent at the day of judgment, and cut off all excuse that shall be attempted to be made (from the thoughts of the greatness of their sins) why they came not to him.

I have often thought of the day of judgment, and how God will deal with sinners at that day; and I believe it will be managed with that sweetness, with that equitableness, with that excellent righteousness, as to every sin, and circumstance, and aggravation thereof; that men that are damned, before the judgment is over shall receive such conviction of the righteous judgment of God upon them, and of their deserts of hell-fire, that they shall in themselves conclude that there is all the reason in the world that they should be shut out of heaven, and go to hell-fire: "These shall go away into everlasting punishment;" Matt. xxv. 46.

Only this will tear them, that they have missed of mercy and glory, and obtained everlasting damnation through their unbelief; but it will tear but themselves, but their own souls; they will gnash upon themselves; for in that mercy was offered to the chief of them in the first place, and yet they were damned for rejecting of it; they were damned for forsaking what they had a sort of propriety in; for forsaking their own mercy.

And thus much for the reasons. I will conclude with a word of application.

THE APPLICATION

First, Would Jesus Christ have mercy offered in the first place to the biggest sinners? then this shews us how to make a right judgment of the heart of Christ to men. Indeed we have advantage to guess at the goodness of his heart, by many things; as by his taking our nature upon him, his dying for us, his sending his word and ministers to us, and all that we might be saved. But this of beginning to offer mercy to Jerusalem, is that which heightens all the rest; for this doth not only confirm to us, that love was the cause of his dying for us, but it shews us yet more the depth of that love. He might have died for us, and yet have extended the benefit of his death to a few, as one might call them, of the best conditioned sinners, to those who, though they were weak, and could not but sin, yet made not a trade of sinning; to those that sinned not lavishingly. There are in the world, as one may call them, the moderate sinners; the sinners that mix righteousness with their pollutions; the sinners that though they be sinners, do what on their part lies (some that are blind would think so) that they might be saved. I say, it had been love, great love, if he had died for none but such, and sent his love to such: but that he should send out conditions of peace to the biggest of sinners; yea, that they should be offered to them first of all; (for so he means when he says, "Begin at Jerusalem;") this is wonderful! this shews his heart to purpose, as also the heart of God his Father, who sent him to do thus.

There is nothing more incident to men that are awake in their souls, than to have wrong thoughts of God; thoughts that are narrow, and that pinch and pen up his mercy to scanty and beggarly conclusions, and rigid legal conditions; supposing that it is rude, and an intrenching upon his majesty, to come ourselves, or to invite others, until we have scraped and washed, and rubbed off as much of our dirt from us as we think is convenient, to make us somewhat orderly and handsome in his sight. Such never knew what these words meant, "Begin at Jerusalem:" yea, such in their hearts have compared the Father and his Son to niggardly rich men, whose money comes from them like drops of blood. True, says such, God has mercy, but he is loath to part with it; you must please him well, if you get any from him; he is not so free as many suppose, nor is he so willing to save as some pretended gospellers imagine. But I ask such, if the Father and Son be not unspeakably free to shew mercy, why was this clause put into our commission to preach the gospel? Yea, why did he say, "Begin at Jerusalem:" for when men, through the weakness of their wits, have attempted to shew other reasons why they should have the first proffer of mercy; yet I can prove (by many undeniable reasons) that they of Jerusalem (to whom the apostles made the first offer, according as they were commanded) were the biggest sinners that ever did breathe upon the face of God's earth, (set the unpardonable sin aside), upon which my doctrine stands like a rock, that Jesus the Son of God would have mercy in the first place offered to the biggest sinners: and if this doth not shew the heart of the Father and the Son to be infinitely free in bestowing forgiveness of sins, I confess myself mistaken.

Neither is there, set this aside, another argument like it, to shew us the willingness of Christ to save sinners; for, as was said before, all the rest of the signs of Christ's mercifulness might have been limited to sinners that are so and so qualified; but when he says, "Begin at Jerusalem," the line is stretched out to the utmost: no man can imagine beyond it; and it is folly here to pinch and pare, to narrow, and seek to bring it within scanty bounds; for he plainly saith, "Begin at Jerusalem," the biggest sinner is the biggest sinner; the biggest is the Jerusalem sinner.

It is true, he saith, that repentance and remission of sins must go together, but yet remission is sent to the chief, the Jerusalem sinner; nor doth repentance lessen at all the Jerusalem sinner's crimes; it diminisheth none of his sins, nor causes that there should be so much as half a one the fewer: it only puts a stop to the Jerusalem sinner's course, and makes him willing to be saved freely by grace; and for time to come to be governed by that blessed word that has brought the tidings of good things to him.

Besides, no man shews himself willing to be saved that repenteth not of his deeds; for he that goes on still in his trespasses, declares that he is resolved to pursue his own damnation further.

Learn then to judge of the largeness of God's heart, and of the heart of his Son Jesus Christ, by the word; judge not thereof by feeling, nor by the reports of thy conscience; conscience is oftentimes here befooled and made to go quite beside the word. It was judging without the word that made David say, I am cast off from God's eyes, and shall perish one day by the hand of Saul; Psalm xxxi. 22; 1 Sam. xxvii. 1.

The word had told him another thing; namely, that he should be king in his stead. Our text says also, that Jesus Christ bids preachers, in their preaching repentance and remission of sins, begin first at Jerusalem, thereby declaring most truly the infinite largeness of the merciful heart of God and his Son, to the sinful children of men.

Judge thou, I say, therefore, of the goodness of the heart of God and his Son, by this text, and by others of the same import; so shalt thou not dishonour the grace of God, nor needlessly fright thyself, nor give away thy faith, nor gratify the devil, nor lose the benefit of his word. I speak now to weak believers.

Secondly, Would Jesus Christ have mercy offered in the first place to the biggest sinners, to the Jerusalem sinners? then, by this also, you must learn to judge of the sufficiency of the merits of Christ; not that the merits of Christ can be comprehended, for that they are beyond the conceptions of the whole world, being called the unsearchable riches of Christ; but yet they may be apprehended to a considerable degree. Now, the way to apprehend them most, is, to consider what offers, after his resurrection, he makes of his grace to sinners; for to be sure he will not offer beyond the virtue of his merits; because, as grace is the cause of his merits, so his merits are the basis and bounds upon and by which his grace stands good, and is let out to sinners.

Doth he then command that his mercy should be offered in the first place to the biggest sinners? It declares, that there is sufficiency in his blood to save the biggest sinners. The blood of Jesus Christ cleanseth from all sin. And again, "Be it known unto you therefore, men and brethren, that through this man (this man's merits) is preached unto you the forgiveness of sins:

and by him all that believe are justified from all things, from which ye could not be justified by the law of Moses;" Acts xiii. 38.

Observe then thy rule to make judgment of the sufficiency of the blessed merits of thy Saviour. If he had not been able to have reconciled the biggest sinners to his Father by his blood, he would not have sent to them, have sent to them in the first place, the doctrine of remission of sins; for remission of sins is through faith in his blood. We are justified freely by the grace of God, through the redemption that is in the blood of Christ. Upon the square, as I may call it, of the worthiness of the blood of Christ, grace acts, and offers forgiveness of sin to men; Eph. i. 7; chap. ii. 13, 14; Col. i. 20–22.

Hence, therefore, we must gather, that the blood of Christ is of infinite value, for that he offereth mercy to the biggest of sinners. Nay, further, since he offereth mercy in the first place to the biggest sinners, considering also, that this first act of his is that which the world will take notice of and expect it should be continued unto thee end. Also it is a disparagement to a man that seeks his own glory in what he undertakes, to do that for a sport, which he cannot continue and hold out in. This is our Lord's own argument, "He began to build," saith he, "but was not able to finish;" Luke xiv. 28.

Shouldst thou hear a man say, I am resolved to be kind to the poor, and should begin with giving handfuls of guineas, you would conclude, that either he is wonderful rich, or must straiten his hand, or will soon be at the bottom of his riches. Why, this is the case: Christ, at his resurrection, gave it out that he would be good to the world; and first sends to the biggest sinners, with an intent to have mercy on them. Now, the biggest sinners cannot be saved but by abundance of grace; it is not a little that will save great sinners; Rom. v. 17. And I say again, since the Lord Jesus mounts thus high at the first, and sends to the Jerusalem sinners, that they may come first to partake of his mercy, it follows, that either he has unsearchable riches of grace and worth in himself, or else he must straiten his hand, or his grace and merits will be spent before the world is at an end. But let it be believed, as surely as spoken, he is still as full as ever. He is not a jot the poorer for all the forgivenesses that he has given away to great sinners. Also he is still as free as at first; for he never yet called back this word, Begin at the Jerusalem sinners. And, as I said before, since his grace is extended according to the worth of his merits, I conclude, that there is the same virtue in his merits to save now, as there was at the very beginning.

Oh! the riches of the grace of Christ! Oh! the riches of the blood of Christ!

Thirdly, Would Jesus Christ have mercy offered in the first place to the biggest sinners, then here is encouragement for you that think, for wicked hearts and lives, you have not your fellows in the world, yet to come to him.

There is a people that therefore fear lest they should be rejected of Jesus Christ, because of the greatness of their sins; when, as you see here, such are sent to, sent to by Jesus Christ to come to him for mercy, "Begin at Jerusalem." Never did one thing answer another more fitly in this world, than this text fitteth such kind of sinners. As face answereth face in a glass, so this text answereth the necessities of such sinners. What can a man say more, but that he stands in the rank of the biggest sinners? let him stretch himself whither he can, and think of himself to the utmost, he can but conclude himself to be one of the biggest sinners. And what then? Why the text meets him in the very face, and saith, Christ offereth mercy to the biggest sinners, to the very Jerusalem sinners. What more can be objected? Nay, he doth not only offer to such his mercy, but to them it is commanded to be offered in the first place; "Begin at Jerusalem." Preach repentance and remission of sins among all nations. "Begin at Jerusalem." Is not here encouragement for those that think, for wicked hearts and lives, they have not their fellows in the world?

Object. But I have a heart as hard as a rock.

Answ. Well, but this doth but prove thee a bigger sinner.

Object. But my heart continually frets against the Lord.

Answ. Well, this doth but prove thee a bigger sinner.

Object. But I have been desperate in sinful courses.

Answ. Well, stand thou with the number of the biggest sinners.

Object. But my grey head is found in the way of wickedness.

Answ. Well, thou art in the rank of the biggest sinners.

Object. But I have not only a base heart, but I have lived a debauched life.

Answ. Stand thou also among those that are called the biggest sinners. And what then? Why the text swoops you all; you cannot object yourselves beyond the text. It has a particular message to the biggest sinners. I say, it swoops you all.

Object. But I am a reprobate.

Answ. Now thou talkest like a fool, and of that thou understandest not: no sin, but the sin of final impenitence, can prove a man a reprobate; and I am sure thou hast not arrived as yet unto that; therefore thou understandest not what thou sayest, and makest groundless conclusions against thyself. Say thou art a sinner, and I will hold with thee; say thou art a great sinner, and I will say so too; yea, say thou art one of the biggest sinners, and spare not; for the text yet is beyond thee, is yet betwixt he and thee; "Begin at Jerusalem," has yet a smile upon thee; and thou talkest as if thou wast a reprobate, and that the greatness of thy sins do prove thee so to be, when yet they of Jerusalem were not such, whose sins, I dare say, were such, both for bigness and heineousness, as thou art incapable of committing beyond them; unless now, after thou hast received conviction that the Lord Jesus is the only Saviour of the world, thou shouldst wickedly and despitefully turn thyself from him, and conclude he is not to be trusted to for life, and so crucify him for a cheat afresh. This, I must confess, will bring a man under the black rod, and set him in danger of eternal damnation; Heb. vi. 6: chap. x. 29. This is trampling under foot the Son of God, and counting his blood an unholy thing. This did they of Jerusalem; but they did it ignorantly in unbelief; and so were yet capable of mercy: but to do this against professed light, and to stand to it, puts a man beyond the text indeed; Acts iii. 14–17; 1 Tim. i. 13.

But I say, what is this to him that would fain be saved by Christ? His sins did, as to greatness, never yet reach to the nature of the sins that the sinners intended by the text, had made themselves guilty of. He that would be saved by Christ, has an honourable esteem of him; but they of Jerusalem preferred a murderer before him; but as for him, they cried, Away, away with him, it is not fit that he should live. Perhaps thou wilt object, That thyself hast a thousand times preferred a stinking lust before him: I answer, Be it so; it is but what is common to men to do; nor doth the Lord Jesus make such a foolish life a bar to thee, to forbid thy coming to him, or a bond to his grace, that it might be kept from thee; but admits of thy repentance, and offereth himself unto thee freely, as thou standest among the Jerusalem sinners.

Take therefore encouragement, man, mercy is, by the text, held forth to the biggest sinners; yea, put thyself into the number of the worst, by reckoning that thou mayst be one of the first, and mayst not be put off till the biggest sinners are served; for the biggest sinners are first invited; consequently, if they come, they are like to be the first that shall be served. It was so with Jerusalem; Jerusalem sinners were they that were first invited, and those of them that came first (and there came three thousand of them the first day they were invited; how many came afterwards none can tell), they were first served.

Put in thy name, man, among the biggest, lest thou art made to wait till they are served. You have some men that think themselves very cunning, because they put up their names in their prayers among them that feign it, saying, God, I thank thee I am not so bad as the worst. But believe it, if they be saved at all, they shall be saved in the last place. The first in their own eyes shall be served last; and the last or worst shall be first. The text insinuates it, "Begin at Jerusalem;" and reason backs it, for they have most need. Behold ye, therefore, how God's ways are above ours; we are for serving the worst last, God is for serving the worst first. The man at the pool, that to my thinking was longest in his disease, and most helpless as to his cure, was first healed; yea, he only was healed; for we read that Christ healed him, but we read not then that he healed one more there! John v. 1–10.

Wherefore, if thou wouldst soonest be served, put in thy name among the very worst of sinners. Say, when thou art upon thy knees, Lord, here is a Jerusalem sinner! a sinner of the biggest size! one whose burden is of the greatest bulk and heaviest weight! one that cannot stand long without sinking into hell, without thy supporting hand! "Be not thou far from me, O Lord! O my strength, haste thou to help me!"

I say, put in thy name with Magdalen, with Manasseh, that thou mayst fare as the Magdalen and the Manasseh sinners do. The man in the gospel made the desperate condition of his child an argument with Christ to haste his cure: "Sir, come down," saith he, "ere my child die;" John iv. 49, and Christ regarded his haste, saying, "Go thy way; thy son liveth;" ver. 50. Haste requires haste. David was for speed; "Deliver me speedily;" "Hear me speedily;" "Answer me speedily;" Psalm xxxi. 2; lxix. 17; cii. 2. But why speedily? I am in "the net;" "I am in trouble;" "My days are consumed like smoke;" Psalm xxxi. 4; lxix. 17; cii. 3. Deep calleth unto deep, necessity calls for help; great necessity for present help.

Wherefore, I say, be ruled by me in this matter; feign not thyself another man, if thou hast been a filthy sinner, but go in thy colours to Jesus Christ, and put thyself among the most vile, and let him alone to put thee among the children; Jer. iii. 19. Confess all that thou knowest of thyself; I know thou wilt find it hard work to do thus; especially if thy mind be legal; but do it, lest thou stay and be deferred with the little sinners, until the great ones have had their alms. What do you think David intended when he said, his wounds stunk and were corrupted, but to hasten God to have mercy upon him, and not to defer his cure? "Lord," says he, "I am troubled; I am bowed down greatly; I go mourning all the day long." "I am feeble and sore broken, by reason of the disquietness of my heart;" Psalm xxxviii. 3–8.

David knew what he did by all this; he knew that his making the worst of his case, was the way to speedy help, and that a feigning and dissembling the matter with God, was the next way to a demur as to his forgiveness.

I have one thing more to offer for thy encouragement, who deemest thyself one of the biggest sinners; and that is, thou art as it were called by thy name, in the first place, to come in for mercy. Thou man of Jerusalem, hearken to thy call; men do so in courts of judicature, and presently cry out, Here, Sir; and then they shoulder and crowd, and say, Pray give way, I am called into the court. Why, this thy case, thou great, thou Jerusalem sinner; be of good cheer, he calleth thee; Mark x. 46–49. Why sitttest thou still? arise: why standest thou still? come man, thy call should give thee authority to come. "Begin at Jerusalem," is thy call and authority to come; wherefore up and shoulder it, man; say, Stand away, devil, Christ calls me; stand away unbelief, Christ calls me; stand away all ye my discouraging apprehensions, for my Saviour calls me to him to receive of his mercy. Men will do thus, as I said, in courts below; and why shouldst not thou approach thus to the court above? The Jerusalem sinner is first in thought, first in commission, first in the record of names; and therefore should give attendance with expectation, that he is first to receive mercy of God.

Is not this an encouragement to the biggest sinners to make their application to Christ for mercy? "Come unto me all ye that labour and are heavy laden," doth also confirm this thing; that is, that the biggest sinner, and he that has the biggest burden, is he who is first invited. Christ pointeth over the heads of thousands, as he sits on the throne of grace, directly to such a man; and says, Bring in hither the maimed, the halt, and the blind; let the Jerusalem sinner that stands there behind come to me. Wherefore, since Christ says, Come, to thee, let thee angels make a lane, and let all men give place, that the Jerusalem sinner may come to Jesus Christ for mercy.

Fourthly, Would Jesus Christ have mercy offered, in the first place, to the biggest sinners? Then come thou profane wretch, and let me a little enter into an argument with thee. Why wilt thou not come to Jesus Christ, since thou art a Jerusalem sinner? How canst thou find in thy heart to set thyself against grace, against such grace as offereth mercy to thee? What spirit possesseth thee, and holds thee back from a sincere closure with thy Saviour? Behold God groaningly complains of thee, saying, "But Israel would none of me." "When I called, none did answer;" Psl. lxxxi. 11; Isa. lxvi. 4.

Shall God enter this complaint against thee? Why dost thou put him off? Why dost thou stop thine ear? Canst thou defend thyself? When thou art called to an account for thy neglects of so great salvation, what canst thou answer? or doest thou think thou shalt escape the judgment? Heb. ii. 3.

No more such Christs! There will be no more such Christs, sinner! Oh, put not the day, the day of grace, away from thee! if it be once gone, it will never come again, sinner.

But what is it that has got thy heart, and that keeps it from thy Saviour? "Who in the heaven can be compared unto the Lord? who among the sons of the mighty can be likened unto the Lord?" Psl. lxxxix. 6. Hast thou, thinkest thou, found anything so good as Jesus Christ?

Is there any among thy sins, thy companions, and foolish delights, that like Christ can help thee in the day of thy distress? Behold, the greatness of thy sins cannot hinder; let not the stubbornness of thy heart hinder thee, sinner.

Object. But I am ashamed.

Answ. Oh! Do not be ashamed to be saved, sinner.

Object. But my old companions will mock me.

Answ. Oh! Do not be mocked out of eternal life, sinner.

Thy stubbornness affects, afflicts the heart of thy Saviour. Carest thou not for this? Of old he beheld the city, and wept over it. Canst thou hear this, and not be concerned? Luke xix. 41, 42. Shall Christ weep to see thy soul going on to destruction, and wilt thou sport thyself in that way? Yea, shall Christ, that can be eternally happy without thee, be more afflicted at the thoughts of the loss of thy soul, than thyself, who art certainly eternally miserable if thou neglectest to come to him.

Those things that keep thee and thy Saviour, on thy part asunder, are but bubbles; the least prick of an affliction will let out, as to thee, what now thou thinkest is worth the venture of heaven to enjoy.

Hast thou not reason? Canst thou not so much as once soberly think of thy dying hour, or of whither thy sinful life will drive thee then? Hast thou no conscience? or having one, is it rocked so fast asleep by sin, or made so weary with an unsuccessful calling upon thee, that it is laid down, and cares for thee no more? Poor man! thy state is to be lamented. Hast no judgment? Art not able to conclude, that to be saved is better than to burn in hell? and that eternal life, with God's favour, is better than a temporal life in God's displeasure? Hast no affection but what is brutish? what, none at all? no affection for the God that made thee? what! none for his loving Son that has shewed his love, and died for thee? Is not heaven worth thy affection? O poor man! which is strongest thinkest thou, God or thee? If thou art not able to overcome him, thou art a fool for standing out against him; Matt. v. 25, 26. "It is a fearful thing to fall into the hands of the living God." He will gripe hard; his fist is stronger than a lion's paw; take heed of him, he will be angry if you despise his Son; and will you stand guilty in your trespasses, when he offereth you his grace and favour? Exod. xxxiv. 6, 7; Heb. x. 29–31.

Now we come to the text, "Beginning at Jerusalem." This text, though it be now one of the brightest stars that shineth in the Bible, because there is in it, as full, if not the fullest offer of grace that can be imagined, to the sons of men; yet to them that shall perish from under this word, even this text will be to such, one of the hottest coals in hell.

This text, therefore, will save thee or sink thee: there is no shifting of it: if it saves thee, it will set thee high; if it sinks thee, it will set thee low.

But, I say, why so unconcerned? Hast no soul? or dost think thou mayst lose thy soul, and save thyself? Is it not pity, had it otherwise been the will of God, that ever thou wast made a man, for that thou settest so little by thy soul?

Sinner, take the invitation; thou art called upon to come to Christ: nor art thou called upon but by order from the Son of God though thou shouldst happen to come of the biggest sinners; for he has bid us offer mercy, as to all the world in general, so, in the first place, to the sinners of Jerusalem, or to the biggest sinners.

Fifthly, Would Jesus Christ have mercy offered in thee first place, to the biggest sinners? then this shews how unreasonable a thing it is for men to despair of mercy: for those that presume, I shall say something to them afterward.

I now speak to them that despair.

There are four sorts of despair. There is the despair of devils; there is the despair of souls in hell; there is the despair that is grounded upon men's deficiency; and there is the despair that they are perplexed with that are willing to be saved, but are too strongly borne down with the burthen of their sins.

The despair of devils, the damned's despair, and that despair that a man has of attaining of life because of his own deficiency, are all unreasonable. Why should not devils and damned souls despair? yea, why should not man despair of getting to heaven by his own abilities? I therefore am concerned only with the fourth sort of despair, to wit, with the despair of those that would be saved, but are too strongly borne down with the burden of their sins.

I say, therefore, to thee that art thus, And why despair? Thy despair, if it were reasonable, should flow from thee, because found in the land that is beyond the grave, or because thou certainly knowest that Christ will not, or cannot save thee.

But for the first, thou art yet in the land of the living; and for the second, thou hast ground to believe the quite contrary; Christ is able to save to the uttermost them that come to God by him; and if he were not willing, he would not have commanded that mercy, in the first place, should be offered to the biggest sinners. Besides, he hath said, "And let him that is athirst come, and whosoever will, let him take the water of life freely;" that is, with all my heart. What ground now is here for despair? If thou sayst, The number and burden of my sins; I answer, Nay; that is rather a ground for faith: because such an one, above all others, is invited by Christ to come unto him, yea, promised rest and forgiveness if they come; Matt. xi. 28. What ground then to despair? Verily none at all. Thy despair then is a thing unreasonable and without footing in the word.

But I have no experience of God's love; God hath given me no comfort, or ground of hope, though I have waited upon him for it many a day.

Thou hast experience of God's love, for that he has opened thine eyes to see thy sins: and for that he has given thee desires to be saved by Jesus Christ. For by thy sense of sin thou art made to see thy poverty of spirit, and that has laid thee under a sure ground to hope that heaven shall be thine hereafter.

Also thy desires to be saved by Christ, has put thee under another promise, so there is two to hold thee up in them, though thy present burden be never so heavy, Matt. v. 3, 6. As for what thou sayst, as to God's silence to thee, perhaps he has spoken to thee once or twice already, but thou hast not perceived it; Job xxxiii. 14, 15.

However, thou hast Christ crucified, set forth before thine eyes in the Bible, and an invitation to come unto him, though thou be a Jerusalem sinner, though thou be the biggest sinner; and so no ground to despair. What, if God will be silent to thee, is that ground of despair? Not at all, so long as there is a promise in the Bible that God will in no wise cast away the coming sinner, and so long as he invites the Jerusalem sinner to come unto him John vi. 37.

Build not therefore despair upon these things; they are no sufficient foundations for it, such plenty of promises being in the Bible, and such a discovery of his mercy to great sinners of old; especially since we have withal a clause in the commission given to ministers to preach, that they should begin with the Jerusalem sinners in their offering of mercy to the world.

Besides, God says, They that wait upon the Lord shall renew their strength, they shall mount up with wings like eagles; but perhaps it may be long first. "I waited long," saith David, "and did seek the Lord;" and at length his cry was heard: wherefore he bids his soul wait on God, and says, For it is good so to do before thy saints; Psalm xl. 1; lxii. 5; lii. 9.

And what if thou waitest upon God all thy days? Is it below thee? And what if God will cross his book, and blot out the hand-writing that is against thee, and not let thee know it as yet? Is it fit to say unto God, Thou art hard-hearted? Despair not; thou hast no ground to despair, so long as thou livest in this world. It is a sin to begin to despair before one sets his foot over the threshold of hell-gates. For them that are there, let them despair and spare not; but as for thee, thou hast no ground to do it. What! despair of bread in a land that is full of corn! despair of mercy when our God is full of mercy! despair of mercy, when God goes about by his ministers, beseeching of sinners to be reconciled unto him! 2 Cor. v. 18–20.

Thou scrupulous fool, where canst thou find that God was ever false to his promise, or that he ever deceived the soul that ventured itself upon him? He often calls upon sinners to trust him, though they walk in darkness, and have no light; Isa. 1. 10.

They have his promise and oath for their salvation, that flee for refuge to the hope set before them; Heb. vi. 17, 18.

Despair! when we have a God of mercy, and a redeeming Christ alive! For shame, forbear: let them despair that dwell where there is no God, and that are confined to those chambers of death which can be reached by no redemption.

A living man despair when he is chid for murmuring and complaining! Lam. iii. 39. Oh! so long as we are where promises swarm, where mercy is proclaimed, where grace reigns, and where Jerusalem sinners are privileged with the first offer of mercy, it is a base thing to despair.

Despair undervalues the promise, undervalues the invitation, undervalues the proffer of grace. Despair undervalues the ability of God the Father, and the redeeming blood of Christ his Son. Oh unreasonable despair!

Despair makes man God's judge; it is a controller of the promise, a contradicter of Christ in his large offers of mercy: and one that undertakes to make unbelief the great manager of our reason and judgment, in determining about what God can and will do for sinners.

Despair! It is the devil's fellow, the devil's master; yea, the chains with which he is captivated and held under darkness for ever: and to give way thereto in a land, in a state and time that flows with milk and honey, is an uncomely thing.

I would say to my soul, O my soul! this is not the place of despair; this is not the time to despair in: as long as mine eyes can find a promise in the Bible, as long as there is the least mention of grace, as long as there is a moment left me of breath or life in this world; so long will I wait or look for mercy, so long will I fight against unbelief and despair.

This is the way to honour God and Christ; this is the way to set the crown on the promise; this is the way to welcome the invitation and inviter; and this is the way to thrust thyself under the shelter and protection of the word of grace. Never despair so long as our text is alive, for that doth sound it out,—that mercy by Christ is offered, in the first place, to the biggest sinner.

Despair is an unprofitable thing; it will make a man weary of waiting upon God; 2 Kings vi. 33; it will make a man forsake God, and seek his heaven in the good things of this world; Gen. iv. 13–18. It will make a man his own tormentor, and flounce and fling like a wild bull in a net; Isa. ii. 20.

Despair! it drives a man to the study of his own ruin, and brings him at last to be his own executioner; 2 Sam. xvii. 23; Matt. xxvii. 3–5.

Besides, I am persuaded also, that despair is the cause that there are so many that would fain be Atheists in the world: For because they have entertained a conceit that God will never be merciful to them; therefore they labour to persuade themselves that there is no God at all, as if their misbelief would kill God, or cause him to cease to be. A poor shift for an immortal soul, for a soul who liketh not to retain God in its knowledge! If this be the best that despair can do, let it go, man, and betake thyself to faith, to prayer, to wait for God, and to hope, in despite of ten thousand doubts. And for thy encouragement, take yet (as an addition to what has already been said) the following scripture; "The Lord taketh pleasure in them that fear him, in those that hope in his mercy;" Psal. cxlvii. 11.

Whence note, They fear not God, that hope not in his mercy: also God is angry with them that hope not in his mercy: for he only taketh pleasure in them that hope. He that believeth, or hath received his testimony, "hath set to his seal that God is true,"

John iii. 33; but he that receiveth it not hath made him a liar, and that is a very unworthy thing; 1 John v. 10, 11. "Let the wicked forsake his ways, and the unrighteous man his thoughts; and let him return to the Lord, and he will have mercy on him; and to our God, for he will abundantly multiply pardons." Perhaps thou art weary of thy ways, but art not weary of thy thoughts, of thy unbelieving and despairing thoughts; now, God also would have thee cast away these thoughts, as such which he deserveth not at thy hands; for he will have mercy upon thee, and he will abundantly pardon.

"O fools, and slow of heart to believe all that the prophets have spoken!" Luke xxiv. 25. Mark you here, slowness to believe is a piece of folly. Ay! but sayst thou, I do believe some, and I believe what can make against me. Ay, but sinner, Christ Jesus here calls thee fool for not believing all. Believe all, and despair if thou canst. He that believes all, believes that text that saith, Christ would have mercy preached first to the Jerusalem sinners. He that believeth all, believeth all the promises and consolations of the word; and the promises and consolations of the word weigh heavier than do all the curses and threatenings of the law; and mercy rejoiceth against judgment. Wherefore believe all, and mercy will to thy conscience weigh judgment down, and so minister comfort to thy soul. The Lord take the yoke from off thy jaws, since he has set meat before thee; Hos. xi. 4; and help thee to remember that he is pleased in the first place to offer mercy to the biggest sinners.

Sixthly, Since Jesus Christ would have mercy offered in the first place to the biggest sinners, let souls see that they lay right hold thereof, lest they, notwithstanding, indeed come short thereof.

Faith only knows how to deal with mercy; wherefore put not in the place thereof presumption. I have observed, that as there are herbs and flowers in our gardens, so there are their counterfeits in the field; only they are distinguished from the other by the name of wild ones. Why, there is faith, and wild faith; and wild faith is this presumption. I call it wild faith, because God never placed it in his garden, his church; it is only to be found in the field, the world. I also call it wild faith, because it only grows up and is nourished where other wild notions abound. Wherefore take heed of this, and all may be well; for this presumuptuousness is a very heinous thing in the eyes of God: "The soul," saith he, "that doeth ought presumptuously (whether he be born in the land, or a stranger), the same reproacheth the Lord; and that soul shall be cut off from among his people;" Numb. xv. 30.

The thoughts of this made David tremble, and pray that God would hold him back from presumptuous sins, and not suffer them to have dominion over him; Psal. xix. 13.

Now this presumption, then, puts itself in the place of faith, when it tampereth with the promise for life, while the soul is a stranger to repentance. Wherefore you have in the text, to prevent doing thus, both repentance and remission of sins to be offered to Jerusalem; not remission without repentance: for all that repent not shall perish, let them presume on grace and the promise while they will; Luke xiii. 1–3.

Presumption, then, is that which severeth faith and repentance, concluding, that the soul shall be saved by grace, though the man was never made sorry for his sins, nor the love of the heart turned therefrom. This is to be self-willed, as Peter has it; and this is a despising the word of the Lord, for that has put repentance and faith together; Mark i. 15. And "because he hath despised the word of the Lord, and hath broken his commandment, that soul shall utterly be cut off: his iniquity shall be upon him." Numb. xv. 31.

Let such therefore look to it, who yet are, and abide in their sins; for such, if they hope, as they are, to be saved, presume upon the grace of God. Wherefore presumption and not hearkening to God's word are put together; Deut. xvii. 12.

Again, Then men presume when they are resolved to abide in their sins, and yet expect to be saved by God's grace through Christ. This is as much as to say, God liketh sin as well as I do, and careth not how men live, if so be they lean upon his Son. Of this sort are they that build up Zion with blood, and Jerusalem with iniquity; that judge for reward, and teach for hire, and divine for money, and lean upon the Lord; Mic. iii. 10, 11. This is doing things with an high hand against the Lord our God, and a taking him, as it were, at the catch. This is, as we say among men, to seek to put a trick upon God, as if he had not sufficiently fortified his proposals of grace by his holy word, against all such kind of fools as these. But look to it.

Such will be found at the day of God, not among that great company of Jerusalem sinners that shall be saved by grace, but among those that have been the great abusers of the grace of God in the world. Those that say, Let us sin that grace may abound, and let us do evil that good may come, their damnation is just. And if so, they are a great way off of that salvation that is by Jesus Christ presented to the Jerusalem sinners.

I have therefore these things to propound to that Jerusalem sinner that would know, if he may be so bold as to venture himself upon this grace.

First, Dost thou see thy sins?

Secondly, Art thou weary of them?

Thirdly, Wouldst thou with all thy heart be saved by Jesus Christ? I dare say no less, I dare say no more. But if it be truly thus with thee, how great soever thy sins have been, how bad soever thou feelest thy heart, how far soever thou art from thinking that God has mercy for these: thou art the man, the Jerusalem sinner, that the Word of God has conquered, and to whom it offereth free remission of sins, by the redemption that is in Jesus Christ.

When the jailor cried out, "Sirs, What must I do to be saved?" The answer was, "Believe on the Lord Jesus Christ, and thou shalt be saved." He that sees his sins aright, is brought to his wit's end by them; and he that is so, is willing to part from them, and to be saved by the grace of God.

If this be thy case, fear not, give no way to despair; thou presumest not, if thou believest to life everlasting in Jesus Christ: yea, Christ is prepared for such as thou art.

Therefore take good courage and believe. The design of Satan is to tell the presumptuous, that their presuming on mercy is good; but to persuade the believer, that his believing is impudent bold dealing with God. I never heard a presumptuous man in my life say that he was afraid that he presumed; but I have heard many an honest humble soul say, that they have been afraid that their faith has been presumption. Why should Satan molest those whose ways he knows will bring them to him? And who can think that he should be quiet when men take the right course to escape his hellish snares? This, therefore, is the reason why the truly humbled is opposed, while the presumptuous goes on by wind and tide. The truly humble Satan hates, but he laughs to see the foolery of the other.

Does thy hand and heart tremble? Upon thee the promise smiles. "To this man will I look," says God, "even to him that is poor, and of a contrite spirit, and trembles at my word;" Isa. lxvi. 2.

What, therefore, I have said of presumption concerns not the humble in spirit at all. I therefore am for gathering up the stones, and for taking the stumblingblocks out of the way of God's people: and forewarning of them that lay the stumblingblock of their iniquity before their faces, and that are for presuming upon God's mercy; and let them look to themselves; Ezek. xiv. 6–8.

Also our text stands firm as ever it did, and our observation is still of force, that Jesus Christ would have mercy offered in the first place to the biggest sinners. So then let none despair, let none presume; let none despair that are sorry for their sins, and would be saved by Jesus Christ; let none presume that abide in the liking of their sins, though they seem to know the exceeding grace of Christ; for though the door stands wide open for the reception of the penitent, yet it is fast enough barred and bolted against the presumptuous sinner. Be not deceived, God is not mocked, whatsoever a man sows, that he shall reap. It cannot be that God should be wheedled out of his mercy, or prevailed upon by lips of dissimulation; he knows them that trust in him, and that sincerely come to him by Christ for mercy; Nahum i. 7.

It is then not the abundance of sins committed, but the not coming heartily to God by Christ for mercy, that shuts men out of doors. And though their not coming heartily may be said to be but a sin, yet it is such a sin as causeth that all thy other sins abide upon thee unforgiven.

God complains of this. "They have not cried unto me with their heart; they turned, but not to the most High. They turned feignedly;" Jer. iii. 10; Hos. vii. 14, 16.

Thus doing, his soul hates; but the penitent, humble, brokenhearted sinner, be his transgressions red as scarlet, red like crimson, in number as the sand; though his transgressions cry to heaven against him for vengeance, and seem there to cry louder than do his prayers, or tears, or groans for mercy, yet he is safe. To this man God will look; Isa. i. 18; chap lxvi. 2.

Seventhly, Would Jesus Christ have mercy offered in the first place to the biggest sinners? Then here is ground for those that, as to practice, have not been such, to come to him for mercy.

Although there is no sin little of itself; because it is a contradiction of the nature and majesty of God; yet we must admit of divers numbers, and also of aggravations. Two sins are not so many as three; nor are three that are done in ignorance so big as one that is done against light, against knowledge and conscience. Also there is the child in sin, and a man in sin that has his hairs gray, and his skin wrinkled for very age. And we must put a difference betwixt these sinners also. For can it be that a child of seven, or ten, or sixteen years old, should be such a sinner—a sinner so vile in the eye of the law as he is who has walked according to the course of this world, forty, fifty, sixty, or seventy years? Now the youth, this stripling, though he is a sinner, is but a little sinner, when compared with such.

Now, I say, if there be room for the first sort, for those of the biggest size, certainly there is room for the lesser size? If there be a door wide enough for a giant to go in at, there is certainly room for a dwarf. If Christ Jesus has grace enough to save great sinners, he has surely grace enough to save little ones. If he can forgive five hundred pence, for certain he can forgive fifty; Luke vii. 41, 42.

But you said before, that the little sinners must stand by until the great ones have received their grace, and that is discouraging!

I answer, there are two sorts of little sinners, such as are so, and such as feign themselves so. They are those that feign themselves so, that I intended there, and not those that are indeed comparatively so. Such as feign themselves so may wait long enough before they obtain forgiveness.

But again, a sinner may be comparatively a little sinner, and sensibly a great one. There are then two sorts of greatness in sin; greatness by reason of number; greatness by reason of thoroughness of conviction of the horrible nature of sin. In this last sense, he that has but one sin, if such a one could be found, may in his own eyes find himself the biggest sinner in the world. Let this man or this child therefore put himself among the great sinners, and plead with God as great sinners do, and expect to be saved with the great sinners, and as soon and as heartily as they.

Yea, a little sinner, that comparatively is truly so, if he shall graciously give way to conviction, and shall in God's light diligently weigh the horrible nature of his own sins, may yet sooner obtain forgiveness for them at the hands of the heavenly Father, than he that has ten times his sins, and so cause to cry ten times harder to God for mercy.

For the grievousness of the cry is a great thing with God; for if he will hear the widow, if she cries at all, how much more if she cries most grievously? Exod. xxii. 22, 23.

It is not the number, but the true sense of the abominable nature of sin, that makes the cry for pardon lamentable. He, as I said, that has many sins, may not cry so loud in the ears of God as he that has far fewer; he, in our present sense, that is in his own eyes the biggest sinner, is he that soonest findeth mercy.

The offer then is to the biggest sinner; to the biggest sinner first, and the mercy is first obtained by him that first confesseth himself to be such an one.

There are men that strive at the throne of grace for mercy, by pleading the greatness of their necessity. Now their plea, as to the prevalency of it, lieth not in the counting up of the number, but in the sense of the greatness of their sins, and in the vehemency of their cry for pardon. And it is observable, that though the birthright was Ruben's, and, for his foolishness, given to the sons of Joseph, yet Judah prevailed above his brethren, and of him came the Messias; 1 Chron. v. 1, 2.

There is a heavenly subtilty to be managed in this matter. "Thy brother came with subtilty, and hath taken away thy blessing." The blessing belonged to Esau, but Jacob by his diligence made it his own; Gen. xxvii. 33. The offer is to the biggest sinner, to the biggest sinner first; but if he forbear to cry, the sinner that is a sinner less by far than he, both as to number and the nature of transgression, may get the blessing first, if he shall have grace to bestir himself well; for the loudest cry is heard furthest, and the most lamentable pierces soonest.

I therefore urge this head, not because I would have little sinners go and tell God that they are little sinners, thereby to think to obtain mercy; for, verily, so they are never like to have it: for such words declare, that such a one hath no true sense at all of the nature of his sins.

Sin, as I said, in the nature of it, is horrible, though it be but one single sin as to act; yea, though it be but a sinful thought; and so worthily calls for the damnation of the soul.

The comparison, then, of little and great sinners, is to go for good sense among men. But to plead the fewness of thy sins, or the comparative harmlessness of their quantity before God, argueth no sound knowledge of the nature of thy sin, and so no true sense of the nature or need of mercy.

Little sinner, when therefore thou goest to God, though thou knowest in thy conscience that thou, as to acts, art no thief, no murderer, no whore, no liar, no false swearer, or the like, and in reason must needs understand that thus thou art not so profanely vile as others; yet when thou goest to God for mercy, know no man's sins but thine own, make mention of no man's sins but thine own. Also labour not to lessen thy own, but magnify and greaten them by all just circumstances, and be as if there was never a sinner in the world but thyself. Also cry out, as if thou wast the only undone man; and that is the way to obtain God's mercy.

It is one of the comeliest sights in the world to see a little sinner commenting upon the greatness of his sins, multiplying and multiplying them to himself, till he makes them in his own eyes bigger and higher than he seeth any other man's sins to be in the world; and as base a thing it is to see a man do otherwise, and as basely will come on it; Luke xviii. 10–14.

As, therefore, I said to the great sinner before, let him take heed lest he presume; I say now to the little sinner, let him take heed that he do not dissemble: for there is as great an aptness in the little sinner to dissemble, as there is in the great one. "He that hideth his sins shall not prosper," be he a sinner little or great; Prov. xxviii. 13.

Eighthly, Would Jesus Christ have mercy offered, in the first place, to the biggest sinners? Then this shews the true cause why Satan makes such head as he doth against him.

The Father and the Holy Spirit are well spoken of by all deluders and deceived persons; Christ only is the rock of offence. "Behold I lay in Zion a stumbling-stone and a rock of offence;" Rom. ix. 33. Not that Satan careth for the Father or the Spirit more than he careth for the Son, but he can let men alone with their notions of the Father and the Spirit, for he knows they shall never enjoy the Father nor the Spirit, if indeed they receive not the merits of the Son. "He that hath the Son, hath life; he that hath not the Son of God hath not life," however they may boast themselves of the Father and the Spirit; 1 John v. 12. Again, "Whosoever transgresseth, and abideth not in the doctrine of Christ, hath not God: he that abideth in the doctrine of Christ, hath both the Father and the Son;" 2 John i. 9.

Christ, and Christ only, is he that can make us capable to enjoy God with life and joy to all eternity. Hence he calls himself the way to the Father, the true and living way; John xiv. 6; Heb. x. 19, 20; for we cannot come to the Father but by him. Satan knows this, therefore he hates him. Deluded persons are ignorant of this, and, therefore, they are so led up and down by Satan by the nose as they are.

There are many things by which Satan has taken occasion to greaten his rage against Jesus Christ.

As, first, his love to man, and then the many expressions of that love. He hath taken man's nature upon him; he hath in that nature fulfilled the law to bring in righteousness for man; and hath spilt his blood for the reconciling of men to God; he hath broke the neck of death, put away sin, destroyed the works of the devil, and got into his own hands the keys of death: and all these are heinous things to Satan. He cannot abide Christ for this. Besides, he hath eternal life in himself; and that to bestow upon us; and we in all likelihood are to possess the very places from which the Satans by transgression fell, if not places more glorious. Wherefore he must needs be angry. And is it not a vexatious thing to him, that we should be admitted to the throne of grace by Christ, while he stands bound over in chains of darkness, to answer for his rebellions against God and his Son, at the terrible day of judgment. Yea, we poor dust and ashes must become his judges, and triumph over him for ever: and all this long of Jesus Christ; for he is the meritorious cause of all this.

Now though Satan seeks to be revenged for this, yet he knows it is in vain to attack the person of Christ; he has overcome him: therefore he tampers with a company of silly men, that he may vilify him by them. And they, bold fools as they are, will not spare to spit in his face. They will rail at his person, and deny the very being of it; they will rail at his blood, and deny the merit and worth of it. They will deny the very end why he accomplished the law, and by jiggs, and tricks, and quirks, which he helpeth them to, they set up fond names and images in his place, and give the glory of a Saviour to them. Thus Satan worketh under the name of Christ; and his ministers under the name of the ministers of righteousness.

And by his wiles and stratagems he undoes a world of men; but there is a seed, and they shall serve him, and it shall be counted to the Lord for a generation. These shall see their sins, and that Christ is the way to happiness. These shall venture themselves, both body and soul, upon his worthiness.

All this Satan knows, and therefore his rage is kindled the more. Wherefore, according to his ability and allowance, he assaulteth, tempteth, abuseth, and stirs up what he can to be hurtful to these poor people, that he may, while his time shall last, make it as hard and difficult for them to go to eternal glory as he can. Oftentimes he abuses them with wrong apprehensions of God, and with wrong apprehensions of Christ. He also casts them into the mire, to the reproach of religion, the shame of their brethren, the derision of the world, and dishonour of God.

He holds our hands while the world buffets us; he puts bear-skins upon us, and then sets the dogs at us. He bedaubeth us with his own foam, and then tempts us to believe that that bedaubing comes from ourselves.

Oh! the rage and the roaring of this lion, and the hatred that he manifests against the Lord Jesus, and against them that are purchased with his blood! But yet, in the midst of all this, the Lord Jesus sends forth his herald to proclaim in the nations his love to the world, and to invite them to come in to him for life. Yea, his invitation is so large, that it offereth his mercy in the first place to the biggest sinners of every age, which augments the devil's rage the more.

Wherefore, as I said before, fret he, fume he, the Lord Jesus will divide the spoil with this great one; yea, he shall divide the spoil with the strong, because he hath poured out his soul unto death, and he was numbered with the transgressors, and he bare the sin of many, and made intercession for the transgressors; Isa. liii. 12.

Ninthly, Would Jesus Christ have mercy offered in the first place to the biggest sinners? Let the tempted harp upon this string for their help and consolation. The tempted wherever he dwells, always thinks himself the biggest sinner, one most unworthy of eternal life.

This is Satan's master-argument: thou art a horrible sinner, a hypocrite, one that has a profane heart, and one that is an utter stranger to a work of grace. I say this is his maul, his club, his master-piece; he doth with this as some do with their most enchanting songs, sings them everywhere. I believe there are but few saints in the world that have not had this temptation sounding in their ears. But were they but aware, Satan by all this does but drive them to the gap out at which they should go, and so escape his roaring.

Saith he, thou art a great sinner, a horrible sinner, a profane hearted wretch, one that cannot be matched for a vile one in the country.

And all this while Christ says to his ministers, offer mercy, in the first place, to the biggest sinners. So that this temptation drives thee directly into the arms of Jesus Christ.

Were therefore the tempted but aware, he might say, Ay, Satan, so I am, I am a sinner of the biggest size, and therefore have most need of Jesus Christ; yea, because I am such a wretch, therefore Jesus Christ calls me; yea, he calls me first: the first proffer of the Gospel is to be made to the Jerusalem sinner: I am he, wherefore stand back Satan; make a lane, my right is first to come to Jesus Christ.

This now will be like for like. This would foil the devil: this would make him say, I must not deal with this man thus; for then I put a sword into his hand to cut off my head.

And this is the meaning of Peter, when he saith, "Resist him stedfast in the faith;" 1 Pet. v. 9. And of Paul, when he saith, "Take the shield of faith, wherewith ye shall be able to quench all the fiery darts of the wicked;" Eph. vi. 16.

Wherefore is it said, "Begin at Jerusalem," if the Jerusalem sinner is not to have the benefit of it? And if I am to have the benefit of it, let me call it to mind when Satan haunts me with the continual remembrance of my sins, of my Jerusalem sins. Satan and my conscience say I am the biggest sinner,—Christ offereth mercy, in the first place, to the biggest sinners. Nor is the manner of the offer other but such as suiteth with my mind. I am sorry for my sin; yea, sorry at my heart that ever sinful thought did enter, or find the least entertainment in my wicked mind; and might I obtain my wish, I would never more that my heart should be a place for ought but the grace, and spirit, and faith of the Lord Jesus.

I speak not this to lessen my wickedness; I would not for all the world but be placed by mine own conscience in the very front of the biggest sinners, that I might be one of the first that are beckoned by the gracious hand of Jesus the Saviour, to come to him for mercy.

Well, sinner, thou now speakest like a Christian, but say thus in a strong spirit in the hour of temptation, and then thou wilt, to thy commendation and comfort, quit thyself well.

This improving of Christ in dark hours, is the life, though the hardest part of our Christianity. We should neither stop at darkness, nor at the raging of our lusts, but go on in a way of venturing and casting the whole of our affairs for the next world at the foot of Jesus Christ. This is the way to make the darkness light, and also to allay the raging of our corruption.

The first time the Passover was eaten, was in the night; and when Israel took courage to go forward, though the sea stood in their way like a devouring gulf, and the host of the Egyptians follow them at the heels; yet the sea gives place, and their enemies were as still as a stone till they were gone over; Exod. xii. 8; chap. xiv. 13, 14, 21, 22; chap. xv. 16.

There is nothing like faith to help at a pinch; faith dissolves doubts as the sun drives away the mists. And that you may not be put out, know your time, as I said, of believing it always. There are times when some graces may be out of use, but there is no time wherein faith can be said to be so. Wherefore faith must be always in exercise.

Faith is the eye, is the mouth, is the hand, and one of these is of use all day long. Faith is to see, to receive, to work, or to eat; and a Christian should be seeing or receiving, or working, or feeding all day long. Let it rain, let it blow, let it thunder, let it lighten, a Christian must still believe: "At what time," said thee good man, "I am afraid, I will trust in thee;" Psal. vi. 2, 3.

Nor can we have a better encouragement to do this, than is by the text set before us, even an open heart for a Jerusalem sinner. And if for a Jerusalem sinner to come, then for such an one when come. If for such a one to be saved, then for such a one that is saved. If for such a one to be pardoned his great transgressions, then for such a one who is pardoned these, to come daily to Jesus Christ, too, to be cleansed and set free from his common infirmities, and from the iniquities of his holy things.

Therefore let the poor sinner that would be saved labour for skill to make the best improvement of the grace of Christ to help him against the temptations of the devil and his sins.

Tenthly, Would Jesus Christ have mercy offered in the first place to the biggest sinners? Let those men consider this, that (have, or) may in a day of trial have spoken or done what their profession or conscience told them they should not, and that have the guilt and burden thereof upon their consciences.

Whether a thing be wrong or right, guilt may pursue him that doth contrary to his conscience. But suppose a man should deny his God, or his Christ, or relinquish a good profession, and be under the real guilt thereof; shall he therefore conclude he is gone for ever? Let him come again with Peter's tears, and no doubt he shall obtain Peter's forgiveness. For the text includes the biggest sinners.

And it is observable, that before this clause was put into this commission, Peter was pardoned his horrible revolt from his Master. He that revolteth in the day of trial, if he is not shot quite dead upon the place, but is sensible of his wound, and calls out for a surgeon, shall find his Lord at hand to pour wine and oil into his wounds, that he may again be healed, and to encourage him to think that there may be mercy for him: besides what we find recorded of Peter, you read in the Acts, some were, through the violence of their trials, compelled to blaspheme, and yet are called saints; Acts xxvi. 9–11.

Hence you have a promise or two that speak concerning such kind of men, to encourage us to think that at least some of them shall come back to the Lord their God. "Shall they fall," saith he, "and not arise? Shall they turn away, and not return?" Jer. viii. 4. "And in that day I will assemble her that halteth, and I will gather her that was driven out, and her that I have afflicted. And I will make her that halteth a remnant, and her that was cast off a strong nation; and the Lord shall reign over them in Mount Zion for ever." What we are to understand by her that halteth, is best expressed by the Prophet Elijah; Mic. iv. 6, 7; Zeph. iii. 19; 1 Kings xviii. 21.

I will conclude, then, that for them that have halted, or may halt, the Lord has mercy in the bank, and is willing to accept them if they return to him again.

Perhaps they may never be after that of any great esteem in the house of God, but if the Lord will admit them to favour and forgiveness: O exceeding and undeserved mercy! See Ezekiel xliv. 10–14.

Thou, then, that mayst be the man, remember this, that there is mercy also for thee. Return therefore to God, and to his Son, who hath yet in store for thee, and who will do thee good.

But perhaps thou wilt say, he doth not save all revolters, and, therefore, perhaps not me.

Answr. Art thou returning to God? If thou art returning, thou art the man; "Return ye backsliding children, and I will heal your backslidings;" Jer. iii. 22.

Some, as I said, that revolt, are shot dead upon the place, and for them, who can help them? But for them that cry out of their wounds, it is a sign they are yet alive, and if they use the means in time, doubtless they may be healed.

Christ Jesus has bags of mercy that were never yet broken up or unsealed. Hence it is said, he has goodness laid up; things reserved in heaven for his. And if he breaks up one of these bags, who can tell what he can do!

Hence his love is said to be such as passeth knowledge, and that his riches are unsearchable. He has, no body knows what; for no body knows whom: he has by him in store for such as seem in the view of all men to be gone beyond recovery. For this the text is plain. What man or angel could have thought that the Jerusalem sinners had been yet on this side of an impossibility of enjoying life and mercy? Hadst thou seen their actions, and what horrible things they did to the Son of God; yea, how stoutly they backed what they did with resolves and endeavours to persevere, when they had killed his person, against his name and doctrine; and that there was not found among them all that while, as we read of, the least remorse or regret for these their doings; couldst thou have imagined that mercy would ever have took hold of them, at least so soon! Nay, that they should, of all the world, be counted those only meet to have it offered to them in the very first place! For so my text commands, saying, "Preach repentance and remission of sins among all nations, beginning at Jerusalem."

I tell you the thing is a wonder, and must for ever stand for a wonder among the sons of men. It stands also for an everlasting invitation and allurement to the biggest sinners to come to Christ for mercy.

Now since, in the opinion of all men, the revolter is such a one; if he has, as I said before, any life in him, let him take encouragement to come again, that he may live by Christ.

Eleventhly, Would Jesus Christ have mercy offered in the first place to the biggest sinners? Then let God's ministers tell them so. There is an incidence in us, I know not how it doth come about, when we are converted, to contemn them that are left behind. Poor fools as we are, we forget that we ourselves were so; Tit. iii. 2, 3.

But would it not become us better, since we have tasted that the Lord is gracious, to carry it towards them so, that we may give them convincing ground to believe, that we have found that mercy which also sets open the door for them to come and partake with us.

Ministers, I say, should do thus, both by their doctrine, and in all other respects.

Austerity doth not become us, neither in doctrine nor in conversation. We ourselves live by grace; let us give as we receive, and labour to persuade our fellow-sinners which God has left behind us, to follow after, that they may partake with us of grace. We are saved by grace, let us live like them that are gracious. Let all our things (to the world) be done in charity towards them; pity them, pray for them, be familiar with them for their good. Let us lay aside our foolish, worldly, carnal grandeur; let us not walk the streets, and have such behaviours as signify we are scarce for touching of the poor ones that are left behind, no not with a pair of tongs. It becomes us not thus to do.

Remember your Lord, he was familiar with publicans and sinners to a proverb; "Behold a gluttonous man, and a wine-bibber, a friend of publicans and sinners;" Matt. xi. 19. The first part, concerning his gluttonous eating and drinking, to be sure, was an horrible slander; but for the other, nothing was ever spoke truer of him by the world. Now, why should we lay hands cross on this text: that is, choose good victuals, and love the sweet wine better than the salvation of the poor publican? Why not familiar with sinners, provided we hate their spots and blemishes, and seek that they may be healed of them?

Why not fellowly with our carnal neighbours? If we do take occasion to do so, that we may drop, and be yet distilling some good doctrine upon their souls? Why not go to the poor man's house, and give him a penny, and a Scripture to think upon? Why not send for the poor to fetch away at least the fragments of thy table, that the bowels of thy fellow-sinner may be refreshed as well as thine?

Ministers should be exemplary; but I am an inferior man, and must take heed of too much meddling. But might I, I would meddle with them, with their wives, and with their children too. I mean not this of all, but of them that deserve it, though I may not name them.

But, I say, let ministers follow the steps of their blessed Lord, who by word and deed shewed his love to the salvation of the world, in such a carriage as declared him to prefer their salvation before his own private concern, For we are commanded to follow his steps, "who did no sin, neither was guile found in his mouth."

And as I have said concerning ministers, so I say to all the brethren, carry it so, that all the world may see, that indeed you are the sons of love.

Love your Saviour; yea, shew one to another that you love him, not only by a seeming love of affection, but with the love of duty. Practical love is best. Many love Christ with nothing but the lick of the tongue. Alas! Christ Jesus the Lord must not be put off thus: "He that hath my commandments, and keepeth them," saith he, "he it is that loveth me;" John xiv. 21.

Practical love, which stands in self-denial, in charity to my neighbour, and a patient enduring of affliction for his name; this is counted love.

Right love to Christ is that which carries in it a provoking argument to others of the brethren; Heb. x. 24.

Should a man ask me how he should know that he loveth the children of God? The best answer I could give him, would be in the words of the Apostle John; "By this," saith he, "we know we love the children of God, when we love God, and keep his commandments;" 1 John, v. 2.

Love to God and Christ is then shewn when we are tender of his name; and then we shew ourselves tender of his name when we are afraid to break any the least of his commandments. And when we are here, then do we shew our love to our brother also.

Now, we have obligation sufficient thus to do, for that our Lord loved us, and gave himself for us, to deliver us from death, that we might live through him.

The world, when they hear the doctrine that I have asserted and handled in this little book; to wit, that Jesus Christ would have mercy offered in the first place to the biggest sinners, will be apt, because themselves are unbelievers, to think that this is a doctrine that leads to looseness, and that gives liberty to the flesh; but if you that believe love your brethren and your neighbours truly, and as you should, you will put to silence the ignorance of such foolish men, and stop their mouths from speaking evil of you.

And, I say, let the love of Christ constrain us to this. Who deserveth our heart, our mouth, our life, our goods, so much as Jesus Christ, who has bought us to himself by his blood, to this very end, that we should be a peculiar people, zealous of good works?

There is nothing more seemly in the world, than to see a Christian walk as becomes the Gospel; nor any thing more unbecoming a reasonable creature, than to hear a man say, I believe in Christ, and yet see in his life debauchery and profaneness. Might I, such men should be counted the basest of men; such men should be counted by all unworthy of the name of a Christian, and should be shunned by every good man, as such who are the very plague of profession.

For so it is written, we should carry it towards them. Whoso have a form of godliness, and deny the power thereof, from such we must turn away.

It has ofttimes come into my mind to ask, by what means it is that the gospel profession should be so tainted with loose and carnal gospellers? and I could never arrive to better satisfaction in the matter than this,—such men are made professors by the devil, and so by him put among the rest of the godly. A certain man had a fruitless fig-tree planted in his vineyard; but by whom was it planted there? Even by him that sowed the tares, his own children, among the wheat; Luke xiii. 6; Matt. xiii. 37–40. And that was the devil. But why doth the devil do thus? Not of love to them, but to make of them offences and stumblingblocks to others. For he knows that a loose professor in the church does more mischief to religion than ten can do to it that are in the world.

Was it not, think you, the devil that stirred up the damsel that you read of in Acts xvi., to cry out, "These are the servants of the most high God, that shew unto us the way of salvation!" Yes it was, as is evident, for Paul was grieved to hear it. But why did the devil stir up her to cry so? but because that was the way to blemish the Gospel, and to make the world think that it came from the same hand as did her soothsaying and witchery; verse 16–18; "Holiness, O Lord, becomes thy house for ever."

Let, therefore, whoever they be that profess the name of Christ, take heed that they scandal not that profession which they make of him, since he has so graciously offered us, as we are sinners of the biggest size, in the first place, his grace to save us.

Having thus far spoken of the riches of the grace of Christ, and of the freeness of his heart to embrace the Jerusalem sinners, it may not be amiss to give you yet, as a caution, an intimation of one thing, namely, that this grace and freeness of his heart is limited to time and day; the which, whoso overstandeth, shall perish notwithstanding.

For as a king, who, of grace, sendeth out to his rebellious people an offer of pardon, if they accept thereof by such a day, yet beheadeth or hangeth those that come not in for mercy until the day or time be past; so Christ Jesus has set the sinner a day, a day of salvation, an acceptable time; but he who standeth out, or goeth on in rebellion beyond that time, is like to come off with the loss of his soul; 2 Cor. vi. 2; Heb. iii. 13, 16, 17, 18, 19; chap. iv. 7; Luke xix. 41, 42.

Since, therefore, things are thus, it may be convenient here to touch a little upon these particulars.

First, That this day, or time thus limited, when it is considered with reference to this or that man, is ofttimes undiscerned by the person concerned therein, and always is kept secret as to the shutting up thereof.

And this, in the wisdom of God, is thus to the end; no man, when called upon, should put off turning to God to another time. Now, and to-day, is that and only that which is revealed in holy writ; Psal. 1. 22; Eccles. xii. 1; Heb. iii. 13, 16.

And this shews us the desperate hazards which those men run, who when invitation or conviction attends them, put off turning to God to be saved till another, and, as they think, a more fit season and time. For many, by so doing, defer this to do till the day of God's patience and long-suffering is ended; and then, for their prayers and cries after mercy, they receive nothing but mocks, and are laughed at by the God of heaven; Prov. i. 20–30; Isaiah lxv. 12–16; chap. lxvi. 4; Zech. xii. 11–13.

Secondly, Another thing to be considered is this, viz. that the day of God's grace with some men begins sooner, and also sooner ends than it doth with others. Those at the first hour of the day, had their call sooner than they who were called upon to turn to God at the sixth hour of the day; yea, and they who were hired at the third hour, had their call sooner than they who were called at the eleventh; Matt. xx. 1–6.

1. The day of God's patience began with Ishmael, and also ended before he was twenty years old. At thirteen years of age he was circumcised; the next year after Isaac was born; and then Ishmael was fourteen years old. Now that day that Isaac was weaned, that day was Ishmael rejected; and suppose that Isaac

was three years old before he was weaned, that was but the seventeenth year of Ishmael; wherefore the day of God's grace was ended with him betimes; Gen. xvii. 24, 25; chap. xxi. 2–11; Gal. iv. 30.

2. Cain's day ended with him betimes; for after God had rejected him, he lived to beget many children, and build a city, and to do many other things. But alas! all that while he was a fugitive and a vagabond. Nor carried he any thing with him after the day of his rejection was come, but this doleful language in his conscience, "From God's face shall I be hid;" Gen. iv. 10–15.

3. Esau, through his extravagancies would needs go to sell his birth-right, not fearing (as other confident fools) but that yet the blessing would still be his, after which he lived many years; but all of them under the wrath of God, as was, when time came, made appear to his destruction; for "When he would have inherited the blessing, he was rejected, for he found no place of repentance, though he sought it carefully with tears;" Heb. xii. 14–16.

Many instances might be given as to such tokens of the displeasure of God against such as fool away, as the wise man has it, the prize which is put into their hand; Prov. xvii. 16.

Let these things, therefore, be a further caution to those that sit under the glorious sound of the Gospel, and hear of the riches of the grace of God in Christ to poor sinners.

To slight grace, to despise mercy, and to stop the ear when God speaks, when he speaks such great things, so much to our profit, is a great provocation.

He offereth, he calls, he woos, he invites, he prays, he beseeches us in this day of his grace to be reconciled to him; yea, and has provided for us the means of reconciliation himself. Now, this despised must needs be provoking; and it is a fearful thing to fall into the hands of the living God.

But some man may say unto me, Fain I would be saved, fain I would be saved by Christ; but I fear this day of grace is past, and that I shall perish, notwithstanding the exceeding riches of the grace of God.

Answer. To this doubt I would answer several things.

First, With respect to this day.

Secondly, With respect to thy desires.

Thirdly, With respect to thy fears.

First, With respect to the day; that is, whether it be ended with a man or no.

1. Art thou jogged, and shaken and molested at the hearing of the Word? Is thy conscience awakened and convinced then that thou art at present in a perishing state, and that thou hast need to cry to God for mercy? This is a hopeful sign that this day of grace is not past with thee. For usually they that are past grace, are also, in their conscience, past feeling, being "seared with an hot iron;" Eph. iv. 18, 19; 1 Tim. iv. 1, 2.

Consequently, those past grace must be such as are denied the awakening fruits of the Word preached. "The dead that hear," says Christ, "shall live;" at least while Christ has not quite done with them; the day of God's patience is not at an end with them; John v. 25.

2. Is there in thy more retired condition, arguings, strugglings, and strivings with thy spirit to persuade thee of the vanity of what vain things thou lovest, and to win thee in thy soul to a choice of Christ Jesus and his heavenly things? Take heed and rebel not, for the day of God's grace and patience will not be past with thee till he saith his "Spirit shall strive no more" with thee; for then the woe comes, when "he shall depart from them;" and when he says to the means of grace, "Let them alone;" Hos. iv. 17; chap. ix. 12.

3. Art thou visited in the night-seasons with dreams about thy state, and that thou art in danger of being lost? Hast thou heart-shaken apprehensions when deep sleep is upon thee, of hell, death, and judgment to come? These are signs that God has not wholly left thee, or cast thee behind his back for ever. "For God speaketh once, yea twice, yet man perceiveth it not; in a dream, in a vision of the night, when deep sleep falleth upon men, in slumberings upon the bed; then he openeth the ears of men, and sealeth their instruction, that he may withdraw man from his purpose (his sinful purposes) and hide pride from man;" Job xxxiii. 14–17.

All this while God has not left the sinner, nor is come to the end of his patience towards him, but stands at least with the door of grace a-jar in his hand, as being loth as yet to bolt it against him.

4. Art thou followed with affliction, and dost thou hear God's angry voice in thy afflictions? Doth he send with thy affliction an interpreter to shew thee thy vileness; and why, or wherefore,

the hand of God is upon thee, and upon what thou hast; to wit, that it is for thy sinning against him, and that thou mightest be turned to him? If so, thy summer is not quite ended; thy harvest is not quite over and gone. Take heed, stand out no longer, lest he cause darkness, and lest thy feet stumble upon the dark mountains; and lest, while you look for light, he turn it into the shadow of death, and make it gross darkness; Jer. viii. 20; chap. xiii. 15–17.

5. Art thou crossed, disappointed, and way-laid, and overthrown in all thy foolish ways and doings? This is a sign God has not quite left thee, but that he still waits upon thee to turn thee. Consider, I say, has he made a hedge and a wall to stop thee? Has he crossed thee in all thou puttest thy hand unto? Take it as a call to turn to him, for, by his thus doing, he shews he has a mind to give thee a better portion. For usually when God gives up men, and resolves to let them alone in the broad way, he gives them rope, and lets them have their desires in all hurtful things; Hos. ii. 6–15; Psalm lxxiii. 3–13; Rom. xi. 9.

Therefore take heed to this also, that thou strive not against this hand of God; but betake thyself to a serious inquiry into the causes of this hand of God upon thee, and incline to think, it is because the Lord would have thee look to that, which is better than what thou wouldst satisfy thyself withal. When God had a mind to make the prodigal go home to his father, he sent a famine upon him, and denied him a bellyful of the husks which the swine did eat. And observe it, now he was in a strait, he betook him to consideration of the good that there was in his father's house; yea, he resolved to go home to his father, and his father dealt well with him; he received him with music and dancing, because he had received him safe and sound; Luke xv. 14–32.

6. Hast then any enticing thoughts of the word of God upon thy mind? Doth, as it were, some holy word of God give a glance upon thee, cast a smile upon thee, let fall, though it be but one drop of its savour upon thy spirit; yea, though it stays but one moment with thee? O then the day of grace is not past! The gate of heaven is not shut! nor God's heart and bowels withdrawn from thee as yet. Take heed, therefore, and beware that thou make much of the heavenly gift, and of that good word of God of the which he has made thee taste. Beware, I say, and take heed; there may be a falling away for all this; but, I say, as yet God has not left thee, as yet he has not cast thee off; Heb. vi. 1–9.

Secondly, With respect to thy desires, what are they? Wouldst thou be saved! Wouldst thou be saved with a thorough salvation? Wouldst thou be saved from guilt and filth too? Wouldst thou be the servant of thy Saviour? Art thou indeed weary of the service of thy old master the devil, sin, and the world? And have these desires put thy soul to flight? Hast thou through desires betaken thyself to thy heels? Dost fly to him that is a Saviour from the wrath to come, for life? If these be thy desires, and if they be unfeigned, fear not. Thou art one of those runaways which God has commanded our Lord to receive, and not to send thee back to the devil thy master again, but to give thee a place in his house, even the place which liketh thee best. "Thou shalt not deliver to his master," says he, "the servant which is escaped from his master unto thee. He shall dwell with thee, even among you in that place which he shall choose, in one of thy gates where it liketh him best; thou shalt not oppress him;" Deut. xxiii. 15, 16.

This is a command to the church, consequently to the Head of the church; for all commands from God come to her through her Head. Whence I conclude, that as Israel of old was to receive the runaway servant who escaped from a heathen master to them, and should not dare to send him back to his master again, so Christ's church now, and consequently Christ himself, may not, will not, refuse that soul that has made his escape from sin, Satan, the world, and hell, unto him, but will certainly let him dwell in his house, among his saints, in that place which he shall choose, even where it liketh him best. For he says in another place, "And him that cometh to me, I will in no wise cast out." In no wise, let his crimes be what they will, either for nature, multitude, or the attendance of aggravating circumstances.

Wherefore, if thy desires be firm, sound, and unfeigned to become the saved of Christ, and his servant, fear not, he will not, he will in no wise put thee away, or turn thee over to thy old master again.

Thirdly, As to they fears, whatever they are, let that be supposed which is supposed before, and they are groundless, and so of no weight.

Object. But I am afraid I am not elected, or chosen to salvation, though you called me fool a little before for so fearing.

Ans. Though election is, in order, before calling, as to God, yet the knowledge of calling must go before the belief of my election as to myself. Wherefore, souls that doubt of the truth of their effectual calling, do but plunge themselves into a deeper labyrinth of confusion that concern themselves with their election; I mean, while they labour to know it before they prove their calling. "Make your calling, and so your election, sure;" 2 Pet. i. 4–11.

Wherefore, at present, lay the thoughts of thy election by, and ask thyself these questions: Do I see my lost condition? Do I see salvation is nowhere but in Christ? Would I share in this salvation by faith in him? And would I, as was said before, be thoroughly saved, to wit, from the filth as from the guilt? Do I love Christ, his Father, his saints, his words, and ways? This is the way to prove we are elect. Wherefore, sinner, when Satan, or thine own heart seeks to puzzle thee with election, say thou, I cannot attend to talk of this point now, but stay till I know that I am called of God to the fellowship of his Son, and then I will shew you that I am elect, and that my name is written in the book of life.

If poor distressed souls would observe this order, they might save themselves the trouble of an unprofitable labour under these unreasonable and soul-sinking doubts.

Let us therefore, upon the sight of our wretchedness, fly and venturously leap into the arms of Christ, which are now as open to receive us into his bosom, as they were when nailed to the cross. This is coming to Christ for life aright; this is right running away from thy master to him, as was said before. And for this we have multitudes of scriptures to support, encourage, and comfort us in our so doing.

But now, let him that doth thus be sure to look for it, for Satan will be with him to-morrow, to see if he can get him again to his old service; and if he cannot do that, then will he enter into dispute with him, to wit, about whether he be elect to life, and called indeed to partake of this Christ, to whom he is fled for succour, or whether he comes to him of his own presumptuous mind. Therefore we are bid, as to come, so to arm ourselves with that armour which God has provided; that we may resist, quench, stand against, and withstand all the fiery darts of the devil; Eph. vi. 11–18.

If, therefore, thou findest Satan in this order to march against thee, remember then thou hadst this item about it; and betake thyself to faith and good courage; and be sober, and hope to the end.

Object. But how if I should have sinned the sin unpardonable, or that called the sin against the Holy Ghost?

Answer. If thou hast, thou art lost for ever; but yet before it is concluded by thee that thou hast so sinned, know that they that would be saved by Jesus Christ through faith in his blood, cannot be counted for such.

1. Because of the promise, for that must not be frustrated: and that says, "And him that cometh to Christ, he will in no wise cast out." And again, "Whoso will, let him take of the water of life freely;" John vi. 37; Rev. xxi. 6; chap. xxii. 17.

But I say, how can these scriptures be fulfilled, if he that would indeed be saved, as before, has sinned the sin unpardonable? The scriptures must not be made void, nor their truth be cast to the ground. Here is a promise, and here is a sinner; a promise that says he shall not be cast out that comes; and the sinner comes, wherefore he must be received: consequently he that comes to Christ for life, has not, cannot have sinned that sin for which there is no forgiveness.

And this might suffice for an answer to any coming soul, that fears, though he comes, that he has sinned the sin against the Holy Ghost.

2. But again, he that has sinned the sin against the Holy Ghost cannot come, has no heart to come, can by no means be made willing to come to Jesus Christ for life; for that he has received such an opinion of him, and of his things, as deters and holds him back.

1. He counteth this blessed person, the Son of God, a magician, a conjuror, a witch, or one that did, when he was in the world, what he did by the power and spirit of the devil; Matt. ix. 34; chap. xii. 24, 25, &c.; Mark iii. 22–30. Now he that has this opinion of this Jesus, cannot be willing to cast himself at his feet for life, or to come to him as the only way to God and to salvation. And hence it is said again, that such an one puts him to open shame, and treadeth him under foot, that is, by contemning, reproaching, vilifying, and despising of him, as if he were the vilest one, or the greatest cheat in the world: and has therefore, as to his esteem of him, called him accursed, crucified him to himself, or counted him one hanged, as one of the worst of malefactors; Heb. vi. 6; chap. x. 29; 1 Cor. xii. 3.

2. His blood, which is the meritorious cause of man's redemption, even the blood of the everlasting covenant, he

counteth an unholy thing, or that which has no more virtue in it to save a soul from sin than has the blood of a dog; Heb. x. 29. For when the Apostle says, "he counts it an unholy thing," he means, he makes it of less value than that of a sheep or cow, which were clean according to the law; and therefore must mean, that his blood was of no more worth to him in his account than was the blood of a dog, an ass, or a swine, which always was, as to sacrifices, rejected by the God of heaven, as unholy or unclean.

Now he who has no better esteem of Jesus Christ, and of his death and blood, will not be persuaded to come to him for life, or to trust in him for salvation.

3. But further, all this must be done against manifest tokens to prove the contrary, or after the shining of gospel light upon the soul, or some considerable profession of him as the Messiah, or that he was the Saviour of the world.

1. It must be done against manifest tokens to prove the contrary; and thus the reprobate Jews committed it when they saw the works of God, which put forth themselves in him, and called them the works of the devil and Beelzebub.

2. It must be done against some shining light of the gospel upon them. And thus it was with Judas, and with those who, after they were enlightened, and had tasted, and had felt something of the powers of the world to come, fell away from the faith of him, and put him to open shame and disgrace; Heb. vi. 5, 6.

3. It must also be done after, and in opposition to one's own open profession of him. "For if after they have escaped the

pollution of the world, through the knowledge of our Lord and Saviour Jesus Christ, they are again entangled therein, and overcome, the latter end is worse with them than the beginning; for it had been better for them not to have known the way of righteousness, than after they have known it, to turn from the holy commandment (which is the word of faith) delivered unto them."

4. All this must be done openly, before witnesses, in the face, sight, and view of the world, by word and act. This is the sin that is unpardonable; and he that hath thus done, can never, it is impossible he ever should be renewed again to repentance, and that for a double reason; for such an one doth say, he will not; and of him God says, he shall not have the benefit of salvation by him.

Object. But if this be the sin unpardonable, why is it called the sin against the Holy Ghost, and not rather the sin against the Son of God?

Answ. It is called "the sin against the Holy Ghost," because such count the works he did, which were done by the Spirit of God, the works of the spirit of the devil. Also because all such as so reject Christ Jesus the Lord, they do it in despite of that testimony which the Holy Ghost has given of him in the holy scriptures; for the scriptures are the breathings of the Holy Ghost, as in all other things, so in that testimony they bear of the person, of the works, sufferings, resurrection, and ascension of Jesus Christ.

Sinner, this is the sin against the Holy Ghost. What sayst thou? Hast thou committed it? Nay, I know thou hast not; if thou wouldst be saved by Christ. Yea, it is impossible that thou shouldst have done it, if indeed thou wouldst be saved by him.

No man can desire to be saved by him, whom he yet judgeth to be an impostor, a magician, a witch. No man can hope for redemption by that blood which he yet counteth an unholy thing. Nor will God ever suffer such an one to repent, who has, after light and profession of him, thus horribly and devil-like contemned and trampled upon him.

True, words and wars and blasphemies against this Son of man are pardonable; but then they must be done ignorantly and in unbelief. Also all blasphemous thoughts are likewise such as may be passed by, if the soul afflicted with them indeed is sorry for them; 1 Tim. i. 13–15; Mar. iii. 28.

All but this, sinner, all but this! If God had said, he will forgive one sin, it had been undeserved grace; but when he says he will pardon all but one, this is grace to the height.

Nor is that one unpardonable otherwise, but because the Saviour that should save them is rejected and put away.

We read of Jacob's ladder; Christ is Jacob's ladder that reacheth up to heaven, and he that refuseth to go by this ladder thither, will scarce by other means get up so high.

There is none other name given under heaven among men whereby we must be saved. There is none other sacrifice for sin than this; he also, and he only, is the Mediator that reconcileth men to God. And, sinner, if thou wouldst be saved by him, his benefits are thine; yea, though thou art a great and Jerusalem transgressor.

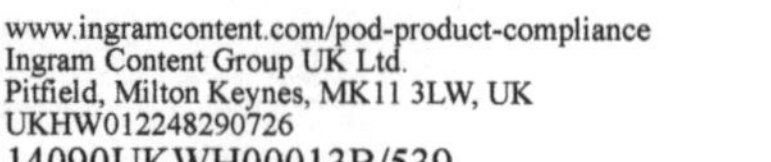

www.ingramcontent.com/pod-product-compliance
Ingram Content Group UK Ltd.
Pitfield, Milton Keynes, MK11 3LW, UK
UKHW012248290726
14090UKWH00013B/539

9 798888 302699